ISBN 978 1 905184 30 9

LMS
JOURNAL.
NUMBER NINETEEN

Contents

One of the late Eric Bruton's favourite photographic locations was the area around Ayres End Lane Bridge, near Harpenden on the London extension of the old Midland Railway. This picture, taken on 6th April 1946, shows a rather grimy Class 5, which Eric felt fully justified its nickname 'Black Five', at the head of a Down Class C Parcels train from London St. Pancras. He recorded the speed as being about 40 mph and the time as 3/40. He also noted that the load was seventeen vehicles, made up of a variety of four-wheel, six-wheel and bogie stock. ERIC BRUTON

Designed by Paul Karau
Printed by Amadeus Press, Cleckheaton
Published by WILD SWAN PUBLICATIONS LTD.
1-3 Hagbourne Road, Didcot, Oxon, OX11 8DP. Tel: 01235 816478

EDITORIAL

In my last editorial I said that this year's Warley Model Railway Club's annual exhibition, to be held at the National Exhibition Centre, Birmingham on 1st and 2nd December, would be a memorable event and that further details would be published in the next issue. I now have the press release and can confirm that it will be held in Hall 5, which has 15,000 square metres of space, the largest hall at the NEC.

There will be some 75 working model railway layouts including five from overseas. Of particular interest to readers will be the celebration of the 60th anniversary of the end of the 'Big Four', focusing on the end of the LMS, promoted by the LMS Society and the *LMS Journal* team. At the time of writing, I do not have any details of what the LMS Society plan other than to say that there will be a large exhibition of models on display.

Graham Warburton and myself will be present but sadly *LMS Locomotive Profile* editor Dave Hunt will not be with us as his son's wedding takes place on the opening day. For my part, I look forward to seeing readers and contributors at what is our annual 'face to face' meeting. Although it is not our practice to announce new titles until they are in the warehouse, I am going to make an exception on this occasion. In addition to *LMS Journal* No. 20 there will be an unnumbered enlarged edition containing some specially commissioned articles, and with luck another *LMS Locomotive Profile* will be launched at the show.

Many readers of *LMS Journal* also take *Midland Record* so it is not out of place to say that we plan to make *Midland Record* No. 26 available at the beginning of December to acknowledge that although the end of the month is the 60th anniversary of the end of the 'Big Four', it is also the 85th anniversary of the end of the pre-group period. I am rather pleased to say that this edition will contain the long-awaited article on Washwood Heath marshalling yard, made possible by Mark Norton allowing me to use some of his late father's pictures.

As many readers will know, Saturday is always a very busy day, so if you wish to avoid the large crowds, Sunday is a better day to attend the club's 40th anniversary exhibition. Graham and I look forward to seeing many of you during this event.

Bob Essery

Articles should be sent to LMS Journal, Wild Swan Publications Ltd., 1-3 Hagbourne Road, Didcot, Oxon, OX11 8DP. Please include SAE with all articles and illustrations submitted for return in case of non-acceptance. Authors must have permission to reproduce all photographs, drawings, etc, submitted.

The Lickey Incline, its Locomotives and Operation PART I – THE INCLINE

by DAVID HUNT & BOB ESSERY

The sound and fury of the Lickey Incline in steam days is epitomised by this photograph of Stanier 8F No. 48422 blasting its way up to Blackwell with a Class H through freight in the early 1950s. The water vapour at the rear of the tender was caused by the continuous blowdown from the boiler that passed through the tender tank before being discharged onto the track. Due to the damage and corrosion this caused to the track, engines were altered from about 1950 onwards so that the water drained from the boiler was discharged into the ashpan. AUTHOR'S COLLECTION

TO many of those interested in the Midland and LMS Railways, the two and a bit miles of 1 in 37.7 incline between Bromsgrove and Blackwell have long held a fascination. Over the years, several pieces have been written on the Lickey Incline but there are many facets of the banking engines and practicalities of how the incline was operated in both directions that have been omitted or confused and which we think would bear further coverage. One of the authors had experience as a young fireman stationed at Saltley in the late 1940s and early 1950s of working trains both up and down the Lickey and both of us have acquired much information on the locomotives that were proposed, built and used as banking engines there. For these reasons, we decided to produce a small series of articles outlining briefly the history and form of the incline, the bank locomotives, and operating details of this short but fascinating piece of railway up to the demise of steam.

In this part we will set the scene with a short treatise on the line's history and construction together with a brief description of the incline and its infrastructure, including the stations at either end, from the time it was opened. We will not, however, discuss the details of track layouts to the south-west of Bromsgrove or northeast of Blackwell apart from the sidings and loops used in connection with bank engines and incline working. As usual, we have tried our best to be accurate but if any reader can add to or amend what we have written, we would be pleased to hear from them.

GENESIS

Situated between mileposts 53 and 55¼ from Derby, the Lickey Incline was built as part of the Birmingham and Gloucester Railway, which was incorporated by Act of Parliament on 22nd April 1836 and constituted one link in the line from Bristol to Birmingham.[1] The first scheme to connect the two cities by rail was floated as early as December 1824 at a meeting in the White Lion Hotel, Bristol, at which it was proposed to build a line via Gloucester, Tewkesbury and Worcester, to be known as the Bristol, Northern & Western Railway. Capital was raised from an enthusiastic group of supporters keen to see Bristol's docks readily accessible to Birmingham's manufacturing output, rather than put up with a week's transit

and high charges by canal, and a survey was carried out by Josias Jessop. Negotiations were underway with landowners but a downturn in the financial markets early in 1826 effectively put an end to the undertaking.

Later attempts were restricted to shorter sections that would eventually be linked together, the first between Gloucester and Birmingham being instigated by Edmund, Joseph and Charles Sturges in 1832. The Sturges were Birmingham merchants and were backed by traders from that city as well as Gloucester & Sharpness canal owners and docks interests, the various luminaries involved forming two co-operative groups for promotion of the railway – the Birmingham Committee and the Gloucester Committee. They employed I. K. Brunel to survey a route and ordered him to find one that as far as possible avoided earthworks, bridges, tunnels and large towns. The first three were understandable requirements for an undertaking that was short of funds from the start, but avoiding large population centres seems a strange principle for a commercial transport project, even with the cost of land increasing almost exponentially in towns. It clearly indicates that the promoters were not actually interested in goods and passengers from intermediate points en route but only with through traffic. Brunel produced the survey with a ruling gradient of 1 in 300 and a route that is said to have been a long way from settlements of any size well to the east of that eventually adopted.[2] The cost of the railway would have been very high, though, and attracting sufficient capital without investors from those intermediate towns that the promoters had ignored proved to be difficult. Eventually Brunel abandoned the project – he had other, more promising fish to fry – and was paid £100 for his efforts, so when the line's promoters decided to look for a cheaper route, another engineer had to be found.

Captain William Scarth Moorsom was the directors' choice. Moorsom was a young ex-army engineer who had served with the 52nd Regiment, gaining engineering experience in Nova Scotia in the 1820s and commanding a detachment to Prince Edward Island in 1829. On returning to England he made the acquaintance of Robert Stephenson and saw the opportunities in railway engineering, so sold his commission in 1832. He surveyed the Cromford and High Peak Railway and,

together with the Jessops, engineered it as well as assisting Stephenson on the London and Birmingham Railway.[3] He was introduced to the directors by his brother, Captain Constantine Moorsom RN, who was Joint Secretary to the Birmingham & Gloucester Railway and destined to become its Chairman from 1841 to 1843.[4] The Birmingham & Gloucester promoters confirmed that their line was simply to connect the two cities without the involvement of intermediate towns and Moorsom's brief was to plan a direct route that could be built as cheaply as possible. To encourage him in the latter aim, his fee was inversely linked to the projected cost of construction. His survey was as close as could be to a direct line, avoiding almost all centres of population and forming a junction with the London & Birmingham Railway at Garrison Lane. In recognition of Moorsom's efforts he was awarded £500 for his survey and retained as engineer for the line. In this he was to take responsibility until the line's opening for mechanical as well as civil engineering with notable ramifications, as we will see later.

The population and merchants of the towns that the Birmingham & Gloucester directors had ignored were not happy at being bypassed and a rival line was projected to pass through Tewkesbury, Worcester, Kidderminster, Stourbridge and Dudley. Fortunately for the Birmingham & Gloucester, the promoters of the new route seem to have been naive and a little incompetent. Despite both local business and newspaper support, not to mention enthusiasm from the populace at large, they signally failed to capitalise on their popularity and the threat their projected line posed to the Birmingham & Gloucester receded. It seems a little disingenuous to say the least, though, that as part of its response to local unrest, the Birmingham & Gloucester prospectus advertised its line as, 'Passing through or near Cheltenham, Worcester, Tewkesbury, Pershore, Droitwich, Redditch and Bromsgrove'. About the only one of the towns mentioned that really lay on the route was Bromsgrove, where ironically there were so many objections to it passing through the outskirts that the line was shifted to the east and Bromsgrove station ended up nearly two miles away in Aston Fields by St. Godwalds. Before the Birmingham & Gloucester bill was presented to Parliament, the Company had to

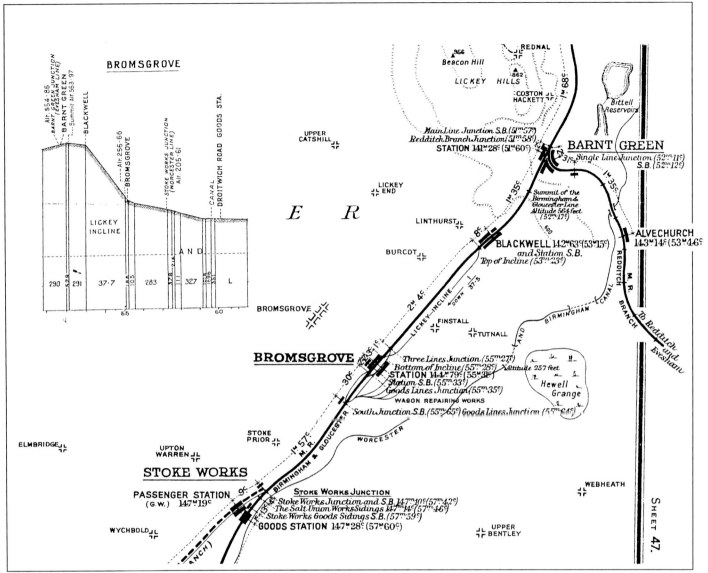

We have included extracts from the Midland Railway 1902 gradient sections and the 1914 Distance Diagrams. Note that the summit is beyond the point at which the banking engines provided 'rear end' assistance.

come to an agreement with the projected Cheltenham & Great Western Union Railway that resulted in a deviation of the Birmingham & Gloucester to within a mile of the centre of Cheltenham at a cost of nearly £120,000. In the mid-1830s that was a lot of money even for a major transport undertaking and the promoters were hard-pressed to find the extra required but they persevered and in the end managed to raise the capital. The machinations of the negotiations, proposals and counter-proposals that this involved are outside the scope of an article about the Lickey Incline, however, as are the various proposals concerning deviations and branch lines to Worcester, and we will leave them to another time.

Since it lay to the west of Brunel's proposed route, the new line's ruling gradient was spoiled by the need to ascend the ridge to the east of the Lickey hills between Bromsgrove and Blackwell and with the steam locomotive still in its infancy, its hill-climbing capacity was severely limited. Brunel and the Stephensons were extremely conservative in the gradients they would accept for locomotive haulage but some engineers were placing more faith in future development and using hitherto unheard of inclinations on main lines. Joseph Locke ignored the prophets of doom and took his Lancaster & Carlisle Railway across Shap and then the Caledonian over Beattock, commenting prophetically that braking power would probably prove to be more problematic than traction when it came to hills. But the climbs to Shap or Beattock summits were eclipsed in inclination by any of the alignments that Moorsom could arrive at for surmounting the Lickey ridge, which led both Brunel and the Stephensons to declare that it would be unworkable by unassisted locomotives. In this assertion they were largely proved correct for the following 125 years. At that time, assistance on banks was normally provided by cable haulage, which was the system first devised for the Birmingham & Gloucester, and when the Company's bill was presented to Parliament it included two separate inclined planes up the Lickey ridge – 1¼ miles at 1 in 54 worked by a 90 hp stationary engine and 1¼ miles at 1 in 36 with a 120 hp one. A slight deviation in the route and alteration of the planned earthworks later changed the Lickey Incline to the well-known 2¼ miles at 1 in 37.7, although at the time of the opening it was

Bromsgrove South could be a busy place in steam days. In this 1949 view, No. 48331 is seen heading a down train, shown by the lamp code as mineral or empty wagons, although the first four wagons seem to have been conveying large pipes. To the left of the picture are the bank engine sidings and coaling stage with 3F tank No. 47565 and the LNER Beyer-Garratt waiting to bank trains up the incline. Note that the Garratt had been turned on the Kings Norton–Lifford–Bournville triangle and was ascending bunker first. On the right of the photograph the Bromsgrove South signal box can be seen with the locomotive depot and wagon works beyond it.   AUTHOR'S COLLECTION

This photograph was taken in August 1933 from the southern end of the up platform at Bromsgrove. At the far right are the Bromsgrove goods shed, associated sidings and goods loop with the well-known signal gantry that used to stand immediately to the south of the station. 'Big Bertha' had just buffered up to the rear of a goods train that was passing through Bromsgrove and starting up the incline.
AUTHOR'S COLLECTION

stated that the gradient was as steep as 1 in 34.5 in places.

Work on the line started at the beginning of 1837 and progressed quickly. There were still rumbles of discontent from some shareholders about the route though, including the concept of the Lickey Incline, and a group of them managed in August 1837 to get an independent report commissioned from Joseph Locke. At that time, Locke was one of the great railway engineering triumvirate, together with Robert Stephenson and Brunel, and when he reported favourably on nearly all of Moorsom's plans it raised the Birmingham & Gloucester engineer's standing immensely. The route, apart from the inconvenience of the Lickey Incline, met with his approval and the only criticism he had of the engineering was Moorsom's intention to use 56 lb. per foot rail on longitudinal baulks, Locke himself preferring 75 lb. per foot rail on sleepers.[5] He assumed, as did everyone else at the time, that the Lickey Incline would be cable assisted and his only misgivings concerned the safety of working passenger trains but Moorsom and the Birmingham & Gloucester Chairman, Samuel Baker, assured him that adequate precautions would be taken. His concerns allayed, Locke gave the Birmingham & Gloucester as planned by Moorsom a clean bill of health and even though doubts still existed about the choice of route, the disaffected group of shareholders was effectively disarmed.

Early in 1838, the Birmingham & Gloucester asked Edward Bury to act as the Company's adviser on the acquisition of locomotives and stationary engines for the line's opening. Among other activities he designed a stationary engine for the Lickey Incline but, as already noted, Moorsom was responsible for all engineering matters until the line was fully open and by that time was convinced that the incline could be worked with locomotives. With his star in the ascendant, thanks to Locke's endorsement of his engineering acumen, the directors accepted their engineer's advice. For some time, though, Moorsom seemed to ignore the problem of just which locomotives would be able to perform the feats of haulage required and it wasn't until the following September that he began to address the situation. The fact that he then turned to Norris in America for engines to work the incline rankled with Bury, as he maintained that Norris's machines were simply

modified copies of his own designs, and relations between the two men reportedly became strained.[6]

The first section of the Birmingham & Gloucester to be completed was that between Cheltenham and Bromsgrove, which was opened to passengers in June 1840 with the Lickey Incline coming into use three months later on 17th September. By the end of the year, Birmingham & Gloucester trains were running into a temporary terminus at Camp Hill but from August 1841, the line was opened to Gloucester Junction, where it joined the London & Birmingham Railway. In its application to Parliament, the Birmingham & Gloucester had applied for running powers over the London & Birmingham into the latter's Curzon Street station. These powers had been granted in the Act authorising the line and as soon as Gloucester Junction was completed, Birmingham & Gloucester trains began running into Curzon Street.[7] At the other end, the line between Lansdown Junction, Cheltenham, and Tramway Junction, Gloucester, was jointly owned with the Cheltenham & Great Western Union Railway (later part of the GWR) and ran over the route of an old tramway. The section was laid with narrow (standard) gauge tracks with the C&GWU laying a third rail for its broad gauge trains and the Birmingham & Gloucester opened its side of Gloucester station in November 1840.[8]

In July 1844, the Bristol & Gloucester Railway opened but trains couldn't run through from Bristol to Birmingham as there was a break of gauge at Gloucester. This caused a lot of inconvenience and ill feeling and the two companies, after a period of wrangling, realised that something had to be done about it. They agreed in January 1845 to combine and form the Bristol & Birmingham Railway but before the month was out had agreed jointly to lease their line to the recently formed Midland Railway. The circumstances and dealing that went on are well known and beyond the scope of this article. Suffice it to state that the Midland took over working of the lines in May 1845, leased them the following July, and the companies were amalgamated in 1847.

THE INCLINE

Through Bromsgrove station the line is on a slight right-hand curve with an overall south-west to north-east orientation and on a rising gradient of 1 in 186, then at the north-east end of the platforms the transi-

tion to 1 in 37.7 begins and the line straightens out.[9] At this point, the 1902 Gradient Sections book gives the altitude of the line as 256.66ft above mean sea level. Immediately beyond the station is the St. Godwald's Road overbridge, originally a stone arch but now a modern concrete structure, after which the line enters a cutting and soon passes underneath the Finstall Road overbridge. The cutting gives way to a long embankment on which the line passes over two occupation arches followed by a bridge across Stratford Road and then on a 1970s structure over the modern A448. About halfway up the incline is a further underbridge that crosses Pike's Pool Lane and the line then carries onto a sandstone ledge with a rock wall and high ground to the east. Another embankment, higher than the previous one, comes next with two underbridges through which pass Alcester Road and Alvechurch Lane, then near the top of the incline proper the line enters a further cutting. From Bromsgrove to the top, taken at the site where the stop board stood for descending trains, the line is straight throughout but then turns gently to the right again and passes through the site where Blackwell station used to be.

Although Blackwell is generally regarded as the top of the incline it is not the actual summit but merely the point at which the gradient eases from 1 in 37.7 to 1 in 291 and the summit is a mile and six chains to the north-east near Barnt Green. The Midland Railway 1902 Gradient Sections book gives the altitude at that point as 563.97ft, the overall climb therefore being 307.31ft, of which about 290ft is between Bromsgrove and Blackwell.

As built, the gradient transition at Blackwell was immediately to the south-west of the station so that the main line and sidings there were on a slight but significant falling gradient towards the incline itself. In the early days this meant that stock left at Blackwell incorrectly braked or chocked could run away onto the incline proper and after several such incidents, fortunately without fatal consequences, the profile was altered in March 1841. The ground was built up so that the 1 in 37.7 was continued north until a level stretch 100 yards long could be gained before the 1 in 291 began. When J. E. McConnell was appointed Manager of the Incline in addition to his other posts in May 1844, he had the profile altered yet again so that the transition was more gradual. The following October he ordered that a shelter be erected at Blackwell for the incline brakesmen.

Despite Joseph Locke's stated misgivings in 1837 about the lightness of the rail Moorsom planned to use, the track in Birmingham & Gloucester days consisted of 56 lb. per foot wrought-iron rail. Most of the line was laid on longitudinal timbers with sleepers used on embankments but despite this general rule, the Lickey Incline was laid throughout as a baulk road. This was changed to sleepered track when the Midland took over but we have no information about when the change took place other than the fact that work on the line in general began in November 1846.

Signalling at first was by policemen giving hand and lamp signals but in 1842 the directors ordered that posts and red disc signals similar to those on the London & Birmingham be erected at Bromsgrove. By the end of 1845, signals for down trains had been erected at Blackwell and a few months later the top and bottom of the incline were connected by electric telegraph.[10] The Midland carried out a complete re-signalling in 1869 with a signal box at Blackwell and two at Bromsgrove. One of the Bromsgrove boxes, initially called East box, was at the station on the up platform whilst the other, known as West box, was further towards Gloucester on the down side of the line beyond the works. The boxes were replaced in 1883, at which time Bromsgrove East box was renamed Bromsgrove Station whilst a couple of years later the West box became Bromsgrove South Junction coincident

with the installation of goods loops. The Station box was replaced again in 1914 and the South box in 1922. Blackwell signal box was replaced in 1897 and again in 1930 when the LMS undertook track alterations described later. Additionally, the so-called 'Lickey Signal' was installed on the up line to split the incline into two sections. This was because of the length of time it took for ascending trains to clear the block, which resulted in congestion at the bottom of the incline but low track occupancy on the Birmingham side of Bromsgrove as far as Barnt Green. The signal was a semi-automatic colour light controlled by a magazine train describer and is discussed more fully later. All three signal boxes were closed in 1969, Bromsgrove Station box becoming a ground frame for the goods sidings.

When the line was opened, the Birmingham & Gloucester Locomotive Works, as well as locomotive coaling and watering facilities and a turntable, were immediately to the south of Bromsgrove station and shortly afterwards, in October 1840, a small two-road shed was built for the banking engines. This was altered and extended over the years and as a three-

road shed remained in use until 1964. Water for the engines was at first taken from a well but this was too alkaline and led to problems with sludge and scale build-up in boilers, so the supply was switched to a stream a short distance to the south. Although this improved the quality of the water supply immensely, by 1844 the flow was becoming insufficient and permission was obtained to tap the stream feeding Pike's Pool a mile up the incline. The pool was on the north-west side of the line and a storage tank was built in the

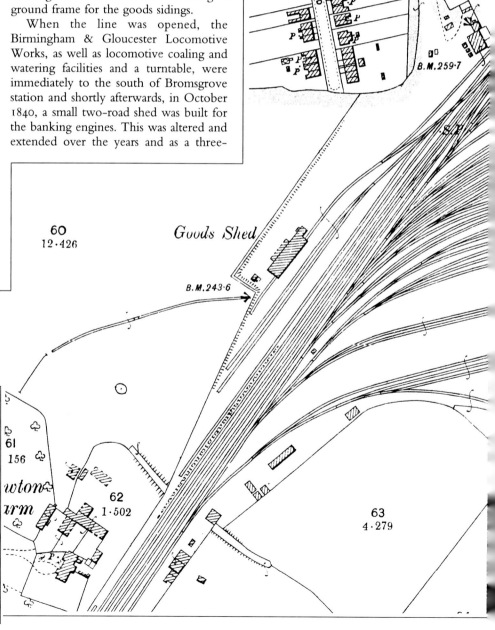

Below: This view of Bromsgrove (not Bromsgrome as stated on the print) station, looking north-east along the up platform, was taken before the First World War. The signal box in the left foreground was installed in 1883 and was destined to be replaced again in 1914. The short transition between the 1 in 186 gradient through the platforms and the 1 in 37.7 of the incline beyond the St. Godwalds Road bridge is apparent. Note how many signs and posters there were in those days. AUTHOR'S COLLECTION

The proximity of the Birmingham & Gloucester Railway's locomotive works to Bromsgrove station is illustrated by this 1969 view. Although taken 120 years after the works had closed as a locomotive workshop, the premises had been used for coach-building and then wagon-building in the intervening period. Most of the buildings were off to the right of this picture, those shown here having been the spring and machine shop alongside the platform shelter with the iron store and wagon-building shop beyond the footbridge. The engine shed was immediately to the right and until 1855 there was an ash pit adjacent to the platform. It must have been a relief to passengers when it was moved nearly half a mile to the south-west. AUTHOR'S COLLECTION

sandstone ledge on the opposite side. There was a goods shed on the up side to the south-west of the station and lie-by sidings were installed on both sides of the running lines. In July 1845, a gas works was opened at Bromsgrove, primarily to heat coking ovens so that the Company could produce its own locomotive fuel but it was also used to light the works and station site.

When the Midland Railway took over the Birmingham & Gloucester, the writing was on the wall for Bromsgrove Locomotive Works. J. E. McConnell left to take up an appointment with the L&NWR in January 1847 and the Works closed the following August, the buildings then being let to the Worcester coach-building firm of Kinder & Johnson. After only a short time they left and the site became a Midland Railway wagon works, although light repairs to the banking engines were sometimes carried out there as well.

At some stage the Midland altered the layout at Bromsgrove station, moving most of the down platform back and putting in a platform road that diverged from the down line at the north-east end. The down line then became a centre road that could be used for through running or for holding banking engines waiting for up trains. The earliest evidence of this layout that we have seen is a photograph taken in 1877 and we suspect that the alterations coincided with the re-signalling that the

Midland carried out in 1869 when signal boxes were opened at Blackwell and Bromsgrove but have been unable to confirm it. Evidence for these changes is conflicting and some authorities have suggested that the three-track layout existed from the line's opening. We find this unlikely for three reasons. First of all, the layout of the down platform and the St. Godwalds Road bridge immediately to the north-east suggests that there was an alteration. Had the station been built with

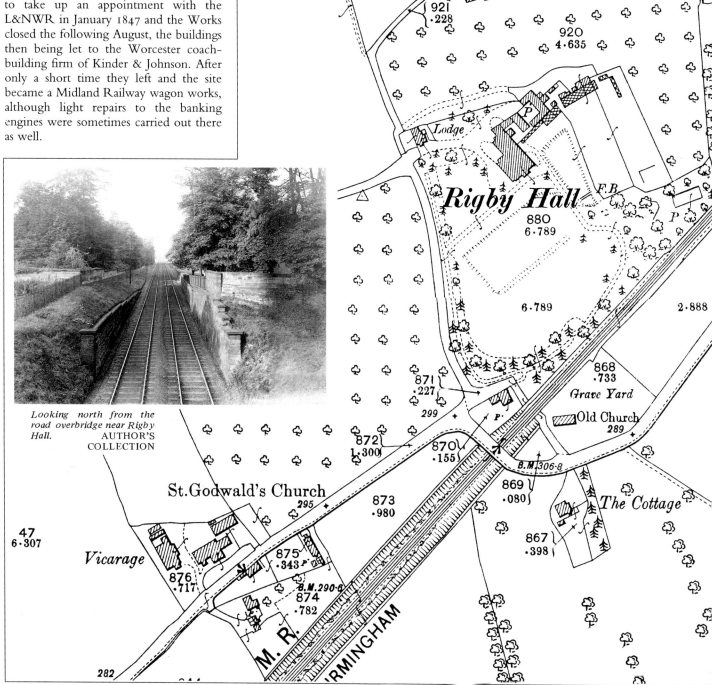

Looking north from the road overbridge near Rigby Hall. AUTHOR'S COLLECTION

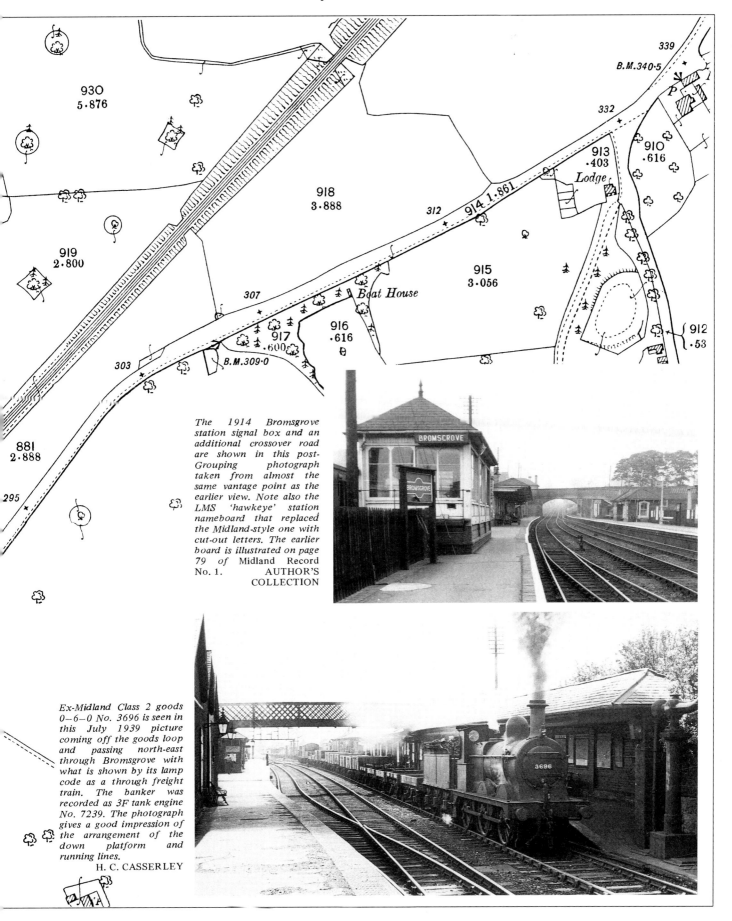

The 1914 Bromsgrove station signal box and an additional crossover road are shown in this post-Grouping photograph taken from almost the same vantage point as the earlier view. Note also the LMS 'hawkeye' station nameboard that replaced the Midland-style one with cut-out letters. The earlier board is illustrated on page 79 of Midland Record No. 1. AUTHOR'S COLLECTION

Ex-Midland Class 2 goods 0—6—0 No. 3696 is seen in this July 1939 picture coming off the goods loop and passing north-east through Bromsgrove with what is shown by its lamp code as a through freight train. The banker was recorded as 3F tank engine No. 7239. The photograph gives a good impression of the arrangement of the down platform and running lines.
H. C. CASSERLEY

three tracks, we would expect the divergence of the down platform road to have started further up the line, to the northeast of the bridge, and the whole of the down platform face to have been useable without trains fouling the centre road. Secondly, the operating arrangements for the line when it was opened did not envisage down trains running through Bromsgrove and so there would have been no need for a through road. The last reason is that descriptions of bank engine working from the line's early days do not suggest that there was a third track. If any reader has concrete evidence to support or deny our assessment we would be pleased to hear from them.

The Midland made several alterations and improvements to the track layout immediately to the south-west of Bromsgrove station including the already mentioned addition of goods loops in 1885. In 1892 the turntable at the engine shed was removed and a larger 46ft one installed nearly half a mile to the southwest, still on the down side of the running lines. On the up side, a siding with water crane, coaling stage and hut for locomotive crews that became known as Bromsgrove South was put in for the bankers. By this time, bank engines pushed trains up the incline rather than piloting the train engine but we don't know definitely when the change happened.

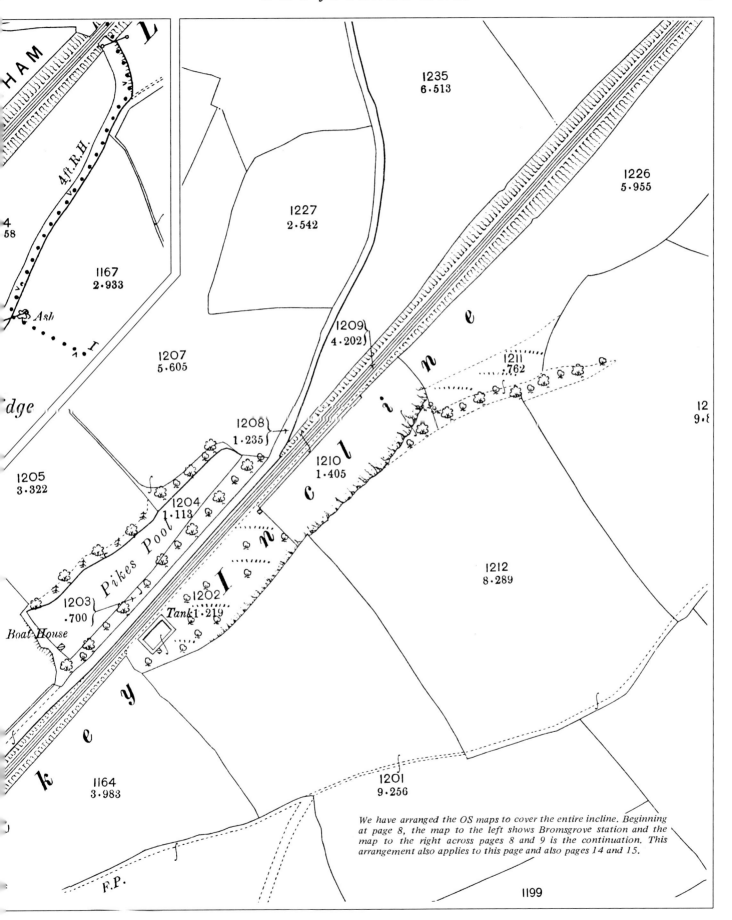

HAM

L

4ft.R.H.

4
58

1167
2·933

Ash

dge

1207
5·605

1208
1·235

1205
3·322

1204
1·113

Pikes Pool

1203
·700

Boat House

Tank 1·219

1202

1164
3·983

k

e

y

F.P.

1235
6·513

1227
2·542

1226
5·955

1209
4·202

e

1211
·762

n

1210
1·405

i

l

c

n

I

12
9·8

1212
8·289

1201
9·256

1199

We have arranged the OS maps to cover the entire incline. Beginning at page 8, the map to the left shows Bromsgrove station and the map to the right across pages 8 and 9 is the continuation. This arrangement also applies to this page and also pages 14 and 15.

Blackwell station had not been built when the line opened. Beyond the top of the incline were a siding and refuge for banking engines on the up side, a trailing crossover to enable the bankers to cross to the down line for descending the incline, and another refuge on the down side. The station was opened in June 1841 between the refuge sidings and the top of the incline with a two-road goods yard on the up side and a siding behind the down platform. In March 1842, a shed and sidings were installed on the down side for servicing locomotives bringing trains to and from Birmingham for the planned change in operating practice following the rebuilding of the Norris 'A Extras', as described later. Water was taken from a well sunk on the site whilst coke came up from Bromsgrove in wagons attached to ascending trains. Empties usually returned by gravity until January 1843 when gravity operation on the down line was banned. When the first altered 'A Extra' *Philadelphia* appeared as a saddle tank shortly afterwards, it was found that its tank was too high for the water cranes and they had to be raised before the engine could use them. In July 1846, gas was piped up from Bromsgrove for illuminating the locomotive facilities.

Once through running by locomotives from Birmingham to Gloucester became normal practice, the need for locomotive servicing facilities at Blackwell fell into abeyance. When they were dismantled we don't know but there is no mention of Blackwell in a list of water stations as at September 1849. The layout at Blackwell then remained unaltered until April 1930 when the LMS undertook the previously mentioned re-signalling and track works designed to give greater flexibility of operation. The running lines to the north-east of the station were splayed out and a centre lie-bye installed for the banking engines, which was taken into use in April 1930. The down refuge was then made into a goods loop in June 1931. Blackwell station closed to goods traffic in 1964 and to passengers in April 1966.

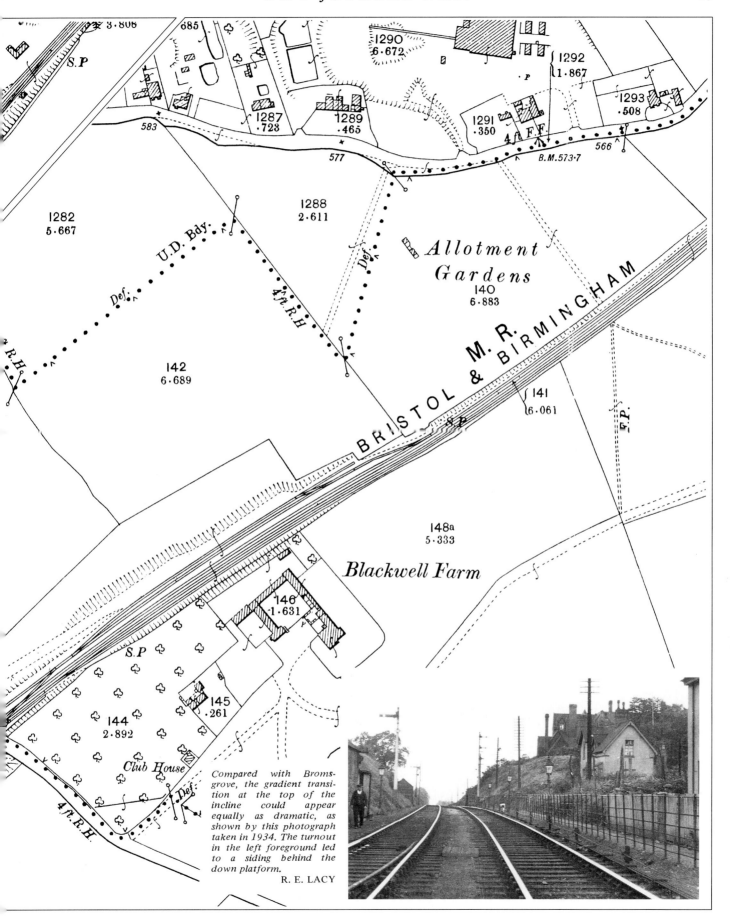

1282
5·667

1288
2·611

S.P

1287
·723

1289
·465

685

1290
6·672

1291
·350

1292
1·867

4 F.F

1293
·508

583

577

566

B.M. 573·7

U.D. Bdy.

Def.

4 ft R.H

Def.

Allotment Gardens
140
6·883

142
6·689

R.H

M. R.
& BIRMINGHAM

BRISTOL

S.P

141
6·061

F.P.

148a
5·333

Blackwell Farm

146
·631

S.P

145
·261

144
2·892

Club House

Def.

4 ft R.H

Compared with Broms-grove, the gradient transition at the top of the incline could appear equally as dramatic, as shown by this photograph taken in 1934. The turnout in the left foreground led to a siding behind the down platform.

R. E. LACY

This view shows Blackwell station, looking towards Barnt Green in January 1907. The signal box was the one erected in 1897 and when the picture was taken there were no canopies on either up or down platforms. The station nameboard was one of the relatively uncommon Midland painted type and fencing was either vertical paling or post and rail. Note the trap point on the siding to the right protecting the down line.   AUTHOR'S COLLECTION

THE 'LICKEY SIGNAL'

As touched on already, the necessity for most trains to stop at Bromsgrove for banking assistance, as well as the subsequent slow progress up the incline, particularly of freight trains, limited the running capacity of the line considerably. This problem became more acute as traffic grew and in 1929 the LMS determined that the signalling arrangements between Bromsgrove and Barnt Green should be altered to increase the line capacity and remove the bottleneck. The cure was to allow two trains simultaneously into each of the up blocks Bromsgrove – Blackwell and Blackwell – Barnt Green. For the latter, this involved the introduction of the Linthurst intermediate block signal but on the incline itself a different arrangement was used. Whilst a discussion of the new signalling could justifiably be seen as an element of the later article on operation of the incline, we have decided to include it here as part of the infrastructure description. Also, although the 1½ miles of up line between Blackwell and Barnt Green are not part of the incline, the signalling arrangements there directly affected ascending traffic, so we will give a very brief description of them.

About halfway between Blackwell and Barnt Green the LMS installed what was known as an 'intermediate block signal' (IBS) or 'advance section signal'. It was operated by the signalman at Blackwell and effectively split the block into two sections. The section of line from the Blackwell up starter to a 'clearing point' 440 yards beyond the IBS was track circuited so that a train had to clear that part of the block before the starter could be lowered for the next train to follow. Normal absolute block signalling applied from the IBS to the Barnt Green home signal. Although such IBSs had been used in several places on the L&YR system prior to the Grouping, as well as on the LMS Central and Midland divisions after 1923, the Linthurst IBS was the first LMS 'standard' installation. At first a semaphore arm was used but this was later replaced with colour lights.

On the incline itself, a two-aspect colour light signal known as the 'Lickey Signal' was installed in July 1930 some 1,500 yards in advance of the Bromsgrove station box up starter. Three hundred yards in rear of the 'Lickey Signal' was a colour light repeater that showed yellow when the signal was at danger and green when it was 'all right'. Colour lights were used rather than semaphores so that during fog or falling snow, no fog signalmen had to be deployed. When considering how the 'Lickey Signal' should be controlled, the LMS had to take into account several factors, not least of which was that owing to the gradient, no train should normally be brought to a stand in case it could not re-start. To satisfy this requirement, it was essential that before a train was cleared to leave Bromsgrove, it was ensured that it would not under normal circumstances reach the 'Lickey Signal' before the train ahead of it cleared the line at Blackwell past the inner home signal.

To achieve this, the signal was semi-automatic, being controlled by the signalman at Blackwell, through track circuits and a machine known as a magazine train describer. The latter replaced the usual block telegraph instruments and showed the class of train as advised by the Bromsgrove signalman – express (passenger), slow (passenger) or freight. Three trains were shown – the leading train on the incline, the following train on the incline, and the next train offered by Bromsgrove. As the leading train cleared Blackwell, those behind it on the describer automatically moved up one place. Depending on the description of the train already in the section and that of the train being offered by Bromsgrove, the describer automatically adjusted the overlap required past the 'Lickey Signal' from 300 to 980 yards before the Blackwell signalman could accept the offered train and the Bromsgrove up starter could be released. In other words, before an express could be allowed to start from Bromsgrove with a freight on the incline, the freight train had to be at least 980 yards past the 'Lickey Signal' whereas with a freight train following an express the distance could be as little as 300 yards. This adjustment of the overlap was achieved by track circuits connected to the train describer. Additionally, the outer and inner home signals at Blackwell had to be off for the leading train before the Bromsgrove up starter could be released.

Further insurance against trains being stopped at the 'Lickey Signal' was provided by an annunciator that rang a bell in Blackwell box when an ascending train reached a point fifty yards before the repeater if the stop signal was at danger. This allowed the Blackwell signalman to take all steps possible to prevent it having to come to a stand. Following trains were protected by catch points on the Blackwell side of the 'Lickey Signal'.

The above is a much-simplified description of the up line signalling arrangements. Further details can be found in the *Railway Gazette* of 13th March 1931 and the *LMS Magazine* for September the same year.

POSTSCRIPT

The Lickey incline is still part of a main-line railway though much has changed from the days of steam. Since the modernisation of British Railways, banking requirements have reduced dramatically, the wagon works closed and the extensive up yard taken out of use. The latter was replaced in the 1960s by a GATX oil storage plant, which itself closed in the 1990s, leaving just a goods loop to the south-west of the station. There are still signs of what used to be with derelict tracks, the old Midland goods shed, and the bankers' hut from later days still visible. In February 1964, Blackwell goods facilities closed followed by the passenger station in April. In 1969 the centre road at Blackwell was removed and a facing crossover and ground frame were installed whilst the running lines were re-aligned and the gradient transition eased so that the maximum speed in both directions was raised from 30 to 40 mph. At the same time, the down platform at Bromsgrove was taken out of use and the up platform made bi-directional. The up line and up platform face were realigned as well as the gradient transition being eased to allow trains both to approach the incline and to pass through in the down direction at 75mph instead of 30mph up and 40mph down as before. This resulted in the track being raised by almost 3ft and a new road over-bridge being built at the north-east end of Bromsgrove station. After many years, the down platform was replaced, the new one opening in May 1990, and a new footbridge installed.

We would like to register our thanks to Graham Warburton for his help with material concerning signalling. In the next article we will begin to look at the locomotives that have been used as dedicated banking engines on the incline.

NOTES IN TEXT

1. The Birmingham & Gloucester Bill was the first to pass successfully through Parliament at the first attempt.

2. The route surveyed by Brunel is not definitely known but is generally accepted as having been well to the east of that eventually employed. To have achieved a ruling gradient of 1 in 300 it must have entered Birmingham from the south-east.

3. William Moorsom had a long and varied career. He was born the son of an Admiral at Whitby in 1804 and trained at Sandhurst. After working on the Cromford & High Peak as well as the London & Birmingham, he started on the Birmingham & Gloucester. When building the bridge over the Avon between Eckington and Defford, he was the first engineer successfully to use cast-iron caissons driven into the river bed with the water then pumped out and the caissons filled with concrete. For this he was awarded the Institution of Civil Engineers' Telford Medal. After completing his contract with the B&G in 1841, he engineered a line from Cologne to Antwerp and gained praise for his twin 600ft span bridge across the Rhine. Also in the 1840s he worked on the Waterford and Kilkenny Railway as well as a line from Kandy to Colombo in Ceylon and on 'Castleman's Corkscrew', otherwise the Southampton and Dorchester Railway. His other achievements included engineering the Ringwood, Christchurch and Bournemouth Railway, assisting on the Plymouth, Falmouth and Penzance lines, and becoming a member of the Institution of Civil Engineers, to whom he read a paper on construction of a viaduct over the Nore near Thomastown in 1852. He was also a published writer with his *Letters from Nova Scotia; comprising Sketches of a Young Country* in 1830 and a history of his Regiment written after he retired from engineering work.

4. Constantiné Moorsom was also Joint Secretary to the London & Birmingham Railway from 1837–1839 and became its Chairman in 1851.

5. Exactly what Locke's terms of reference were with regard to the route planned by Moorsom and the Birmingham & Gloucester directors is not clear. Whatever they were, it would seem that he accepted the principle of avoiding population centres and obviously saw the line as a trunk route in keeping with his own major projects at the time.

6. Bury was probably justified in his assertions. In the early 1830s he had exported locomotives to America that had been examined by Norris, who then adapted the basic design for the lighter, more poorly laid track generally found in that country. The result was the 4–2–0.

7. The running powers granted in the Birmingham & Gloucester Act of 1836 gave the Company the right to use the London & Birmingham's Curzon Street station or 'any future terminus of that Company in or near Birmingham'. This was the means by which the Midland later gained access to New Street.

8. Even after the Act of Parliament was passed, the Gloucester Committee wanted to amend Moorsom's plans and to make the B&G a broad gauge line. At one stage, the directors seriously considered a recommendation by Edward Bury that a gauge of 5ft 6in be adopted, which would have led to even more interesting transhipment chaos at Birmingham similar to that which happened for a few years at Gloucester. At Moorsom's behest though, standard gauge was finally decided on in December 1836.

9. Although virtually all references to, and diagrams of, the incline show the gradient as a constant 1 in 37.7, a Birmingham & Gloucester Railway report on the testing of a Norris locomotive in June 1840 states that the gradient was in places as steep as 1 in 34.5 and a Midland Railway diagram from 1880 gives it as 1 in 36.5. The 1914 distance diagram shows 1 in 37.5 whilst the gradient section has the familiar 1 in 37.7.

10. The Midland Railway issued a comprehensive instruction about the method to be adopted to distinguish between different lines of rails by the terms UP and DOWN. This instruction was dated 1857 and an article in *Midland Record* No. 21 explains how it came about.

The day I started to finalise this edition, with half a page to fill, I also received this letter from reader G. M. Kerr. If any readers can comment further, I would be pleased to hear from them. Finally, I have included a picture of No. 7953, taken some years after its trials on the Lickey Incline. Editor

LMS Locomotive Allocations
I have read with interest the articles by William Dunn on LMS locomotive allocations in *LMS Journal* Nos. 1 and 12 (is he a relative of J. M. Dunn?)*. My particular interest is the eight-coupled tank classes, and R. Hadley's article in issue No. 1 on the LNWR 0–8–4 tanks contained much interesting material.

Elsewhere, I have read that in 1929/30 No. 7953 of this class was tried on Lickey Incline banking duties but was not successful. Despite living in Worcestershire for some years, I have found no record of how it performed and assume it was unsuitable for the continuous hard steaming required for this duty. Also perhaps the Bromsgrove loco men made sure it wasn't up to the job as it could have replaced two 0–6–0 tanks and a set of men might have been made redundant! A former Hereford locoman I know gave this as a reason for the trial of GWR 2–8–0T 5226 being terminated 30 years later, despite its apparent success on the Lickey'.†

The allocations shown for the 0–8–2 tanks by Mr. Dunn in issue No. 12 show them all, as expected, at ex-LNWR sheds. Other sources suggest that, in 1927, No. 7885 was tried on banking duties at Copy Pit on the former L&YR system, while, in 1929, 25 were on the Western Division (ex-LNWR), four on the Midland and one on the Central.

I cannot find any other reference to a Midland Division allocation and have no idea which shed or sheds were involved. As for Central Division, did this include Huddersfield, as it was coded 25B in the Wakefield District, although ex-LNWR? My contacts at Todmorden have no information about Copy Pit banking, and to which shed No. 7885 was allocated when it was so employed. This was usually a Rose Grove duty. Mr. Dunn shows 7885 at Carnforth in 1926.

I would be interested to know if you or any of the readers can shed (sorry!) any light on these points.

Geoffrey M. Kerr
Todmorden

*No. W. Dunn is from Stoke-on-Trent.
† I agree. At that time the policy of cost reduction was largely about reducing the number of men employed, so many railwaymen worked on 'job preservation'.

(Editor)

No. 7953, taken some years after its trials on the Lickey Incline.
COLLECTION R. J. ESSERY

Although photographed a few years before the author worked over this section of line, there were few changes to be seen for a number of years. This 12th July 1939 view was taken at Blackwell and shows a Class 4F No. 4433 on a down Express freight train.

H. C. CASSERLEY

HOW IT WAS DONE
PART FIVE
Widening experience in the Control Link

by TERRY ESSERY

FROM the relative routine and orderliness of Saltley's Bank Pilot link, firemen were then promoted into the Control link, which could not be more opposite in both respects. Instead of having rostered jobs, as was the case in most other links Control link crews had only rostered times and, even then, firemen were often 'borrowed' for some turn that was short of a fireman and therefore they were parted from their regular mate on that particular day. The Control link was really a pool of spare men, drip fed into the system all round the clock, from which individual drivers, firemen or complete crews could be drawn to fulfil demands as they arose. At large sheds hardly an hour passed without some footplate man failing to arrive at his booked time and quite often for some very valid reason – sudden sickness, transport failure, over-sleeping, domestic crisis, freak weather or deliberately going absent, with the latter reason being not at all uncommon amongst unmarried firemen, particularly at weekends. With so many contingencies regularly occurring, it can readily be seen why crews frequently became split apart and individuals could go days without seeing their booked mates.

However, the principal *raison d'être* was to supply relief crews for any purpose, to go anywhere they were needed, and this encompassed every conceivable type of duty. Although passenger services frequently suffered some delays, in all fairness most were insignificant and adequately covered by their normal booked relief. Only when a major incident occurred, such as locomotive failure, accident or when assistance was required from a pilot engine, did Control link men become involved. In these instances, no regular men were rostered to cover what was in effect an emergency. Understandably, all freight workings were subject to a sort of pecking order with fully-fitted trains, including parcels and empty stock, taking top priority. Below these came the other express freights with running speed and importance usually the main criteria to ensure a less interrupted passage. On top of this pile were the semi-fitted with at least one-third of its vehicles possessing self-acting brakes led by the driver. Such trains were restricted to a maximum of 50mph but on pitch black nights without benefit from speedometers, few drivers could judge this accurately on all occasions, so often speeds in excess were attained quite unwittingly, particularly when engines were in good fettle and smooth riding. These semi-fitted, together with the next category down, the so called 'Maltese Crosses', with at least four continuously braked vehicles next to the engine, were the most disliked by guards. With quite formidable braking power available (many vans were equipped with quick-acting brake valves that could allow large volumes of air into their brake cylinders almost instantaneously), behind this block of braked vehicles came 30 or so loose-coupled ones with a considerable gap between each. These had the potential for violent 'buffering up' following a sudden brake application, thus the apprehension of guards can be more easily understood. Most drivers were very conscious of their guard's vulnerability on these trains and, in order to avoid injury, they were very punctilious with their braking technique. The situation was made worse by widely varying brake efficiency that tended to cause uneven retardation and consequently ripples and surges. Admittedly these surges also occurred with fully-fitted trains during firm braking, but because the vehicles were held tightly together by screw or shortened instanter couplings, the buffeting effects on guards were less severe.

Next in line to the Maltese Crosses came non-fitted express through freights. These were titled 'class F' (later 5) and often ran the lengthier journeys between major marshalling centres carrying non-perishable goods. Sometimes crews were diagrammed to lodge at their destinations on these turns but more frequently these potentially long-distance, long-duration freights were scheduled to have crews relieved at convenient intervals along the route. Next in line to the class Fs were the even more numerous class H non-fitted through freights. They, too, could also cover considerable journeys, but, because of their lower priority and speed, they frequently became subject to many delays and therefore crews regularly needed relief after travelling relatively short distances. Still lower down the pecking order came through mineral traffic and because of their leisurely acceleration up to a slow maximum speed, together with extended braking distances, wide paths with generous timings were needed between other movements. However, in moments of great urgency such as fuel shortages in power stations or gas works, a higher priority was grudgingly granted that unfortunately resulted in unavoidable delays to other traffic. Local, short-distance trip work was slotted in where possible, as were indeed light engines, but because of the latter's rapid acceleration and braking, they caused few problems.

Saltley's Control link therefore provided men that could cover every possible requirement using just about every type of locomotive from Class 1F 0–6–0 tanks to 2–6–0 0–6–2 Beyer-Garratts and Class 2P 4–4–0s to 4–6–0 5XP express passenger engines. Such variety on a daily basis provided an ideal platform for aspiring young firemen to expand their knowledge, stamina, physical strength and their firing technique. Occasionally they were the only ones available to fill an emergency and then regrettably these relatively inexperienced lads were dropped into a situation way beyond their capability. How they responded to this gave their drivers a good inkling of not only their overall character, but also their present physical prowess. The driver's consequent opinion soon circulated around other drivers and foremen alike and, perhaps not surprisingly, the willingness of firemen to work flat out until they dropped was valued far more than a glib tongue and short duration skill with a shovel.

Although emergencies did occur and during summer quite a number of holiday specials required manning, where possible the more experienced firemen were allocated to these. A long hard day spent out of their depth did little to further firemen's self esteem and although a degree of embarrassment is necessary in everyone's lives to keep egos in check, too much can harm self-confidence. Young firemen could not always be protected from every situation because with any type of machinery, failures or at least difficulties can happen and with steam engines it was traditional to keep them going to the end of the run if humanly possible. On many occasions engines have been afflicted en route by all manner of problems for which they could quite reasonably be failed, but such a course was unthinkable for most crews. Broken piston or valve rings, leaking superheater elements, blowing gland packings can all increase steam consumption and therefore the firing rate by anything from 10–100%. These defects could well be accompanied by poor quality fuel having to be brought forward from the back of the tender. Endeavouring to keep time in these circumstances required firemen's activity rates to be stepped up to way beyond acceptable levels. What these young heroes achieved in such situations was nothing short of remarkable and, although so exhausted with these efforts they had barely the strength to climb down from the footplate on reaching their destination, few complained.

The pleasure and pride of overcoming formidable adversity and achieving far beyond what was expected from them, more than compensated for all their pain and suffering. This feeling of pride, job satisfaction and fulfilment became almost an addiction and, once rooted in their systems, permitted only total dedication and indeed became a way of life. Each new generation of enginemen carried on these traditions of single-minded responsibility and professional pride for the very same reasons as their forebears – the pleasure and gratification of succeeding when all the odds were stacked heavily against them. There were, of course, occasions when a number of problems combined to present insurmountable obstacles that were too difficult for the fireman to overcome. Fortunately in the Control link, drivers were still relatively young and active and could weigh in to retrieve a developing crisis. In these instances firemen received first-class practical instruction in methodology that was rarely forgotten.

However, the vast majority of Control link work centred on local relief of freight trains, particularly at night when fewer passenger trains occupied the main lines. During the period between the autumnal equinox in September and the vernal equinox in March, nights are longer than days, reaching maximum misery in late December when nearly 16 hours of darkness have to be endured. In the depth of winter, therefore, it was quite possible for crews to rarely see quality daylight for weeks on end, which was extremely depressing and particularly rough on those suffering from what is now known as 'seasonal affective disorder'. This, though, was just another hardship to overcome and the limited-range operations of the Control link were again ideal to learn how to deal with these difficulties on a daily basis. Because Saltley was essentially a freight depot and far more freight movements took place at night, the sooner firemen became comfortable working in these conditions the better. It was undoubtedly very taxing for all concerned, for winter nights were often accompanied by foul weather, but these additional hardships were unquestionably character building and did much to reinforce that which had been acquired in the previous two links.

It is impossible to state which was the most important benefit learned during their stay in the Control link, but experience of working on the wide variety of locomotives operating over their region must surely come very near the top. These young firemen were, of course, familiar and reasonably competent with the Class 3F 0–6–0 tender engines allocated to bank pilot work, but they had little or no experience at all of the ubiquitous Class 4F 0–6–0s now encountered every day on every type of duty. That they did so was hardly surprising since no fewer than 772 examples had been built between 1911 and 1941, indicating that 4Fs were rather useful machines. It must be admitted, though, that despite having the superheated version of the same G7 boiler and identical wheel sizes and axle spacing, firemen received quite a shock on first acquaintance. This shock would not be concerned with general layout since the disposition of pipe-work and gauges were very similar to that of a 3F except that there was no sight-feed lubricator; on the other hand, though, most were provided with carriage-warming apparatus complete with steam pressure gauge. The fireman's seat-cum-locker was just as generous and useful, tenders were larger and better equipped with lockers and had the luxury of rear-mounted steps, but then they would have become well acquainted with all these features during their time in the shed link. No, the shock came when they first had to perform some serious firing in order to try and supply a heavy and sustained demand for steam immediately after a long period of standing idle.

The Class 4Fs always appeared to be larger engines than 3Fs, mainly because of a boiler pitched 10 inches higher and a longer smokebox. Nevertheless, boiler, firebox and grate shared identical measurements and because of this similarity firemen tended to initially use the same techniques while anticipating similar results. That they did not perform the same was due to a number of factors, but it soon had the more inquisitive asking questions and then for advice. These factors were partly due to the particular design features of 4Fs and partly due to the conditions in which they were operating. Both combined to give these relatively inexperienced firemen wonderful lessons on how physics, chemistry and engineering all have to be in harmony before steam locomotives perform effectively and efficiently. Understanding the different characteristics of the superheated G7 boilers helped firemen to cope to a certain degree, but even the most comprehensive grasp of prevailing local conditions could do absolutely nothing to alter these features and they had to be tackled by using new methods.

G7 boilers had 21 large-diameter superheater flues which reduced the heating surface from 1388.25 sq ft to 1167.25 sq ft – 19% less. Admittedly the superheater elements gave another 252.75 sq ft, but these did not boil water in the accepted sense, they only added energy to that already produced and to function efficiently they had to be maintained at high temperatures. With this condition achieved, less weight of steam was required to fill cylinders for a given power output while enhanced flow properties and better distribution through valve ports, etc, more than compensated for lower production rates, thus giving 4Fs improved economy. Unfortunately, in the prevailing operating climate at that time, ideal conditions were rarely achieved and therefore 4Fs usually struggled because superheaters never had a chance to get really hot and what steam was produced had to fill their larger cylinders. In other words, they consumed more steam when cold and yet their boilers produced less, a problem that required experience to overcome.

It is difficult to imagine today just how much traffic was handled by railways 50 years ago when the system was, in any case, much more extensive. Most of the nation's energy requirements were supplied by coal, pretty well every home was heated by open fires, while the railways themselves consumed millions of tons per annum, and it was all moved around on open wagons in never-ending processions of mineral trains. There was no North Sea gas; it all had to be manufactured locally in town gas works. The by-products of this daily manufacturing process were coke and a variety of chemicals derived from coal gas tar, which then, of course, required more processions of trains for distribution around the country. Likewise, electricity generating plants were widely scattered throughout the length and breadth of the land, coal fired and with a continual appetite for trainloads of fuel. Half a century ago, winters were often much harsher than at the present time so understandably energy demands rose accordingly and therefore new members of the Control link at that time of year found conditions far from easy. Already congested lines became considerably worse during severe cold spells since freight yards could only handle a finite quantity of trains in 24 hours. Queuing outside on goods lines was inevitable and when these lines filled, approaching trains had to be placed in any intermediate loop.

With original train crews stranded on these goods lines, already working overtime and without food or drink, Control link men came to the rescue. Most mineral trains arrived from north-east of Birmingham, many originating from Toton; some were passing through, some for exchange onto the Great Western at Bordesley and a sizeable number destined for local consumption. Relief could take place as far afield as Water Orton some 7 miles from Saltley, although usually rather closer at Castle Bromwich, Bromford or Washwood Heath. Occasionally one of three MPD buses might provide transport but more often than not it was a case of walking, taking no more than the prescribed time allowance by public roads. Needless to say, men preferred to hitch lifts on any light engine or train travelling in the desired direction and this mixture of riding and walking on 'company' land was much more popular, especially in adverse weather conditions.

Taking over an engine that had been out on the road for 10 hours or longer (sometimes much longer) on a cold wet night was never a joyful experience. Fires were usually full of ash and clinker, as indeed were ashpans with ash and smokeboxes with char. The fireman may have made an attempt at cleaning his fire earlier in the journey but that was probably prior to their dash from the previous loop to prevent inertia on the goods line and so by now it would be as bad as before. Coal also needed to be worked forward, but since movement, if any, only took the form of a series of walking pace crawls of just one train length, little was required to keep the water boiling. It was not unknown for relief crews to be relieved themselves some eight hours later having travelled only 2 or 3 miles; needless to say, by the time trains eventually arrived at their destinations, locomotive fires were in an appalling condition and could barely make sufficient steam to take them to the shed. However, this could also be regarded as a positive experience since it gave both crew members the opportunity of working as a team in order to 'nurse' the engine back to base without delaying other traffic. As firemen progressed through the Control links they frequently had to practise this art of nursing when faced with adverse conditions, so the sooner it was learned the better.

Although much of the Control link's work involved short duration relief jobs, usually operating within 6–7 miles of Saltley MPD when two or three engines could be brought back to the shed and disposed of, there were longer, more interesting turns as well. From time to time, west-bound freights became excessively delayed and their crews needed relief, in which case Control link men enjoyed the prospect of a longer run. Often this was only as far as Bromsgrove where a commodious relief cabin, watering facilities and even an adjacent loco shed at the base of the Lickey Incline, made it an ideal relief point for trains travelling in either direction. On the up line, all trains stopped in order that bankers were able to take up position at their rear, while at the same time using the delay to top-up depleted tanks with water. On the down line, all non-fitted trains were obliged to halt in order to pick up brakes pinned down at Blackwell, the incline's summit. Again, while this lengthy process was taking place, crews took advantage of ideally placed water columns adjacent to the relief cabin. Although only very rarely, sometimes they were required to man the train through to Ashchurch, Cheltenham, Gloucester or Worcester via Droitwich.

Then the fireman might indulge in a quick, frantic fire-cleaning session and/or getting coal forward while the tank was filling. Motive power on these trains most commonly took the form of a Class 4F although 3Fs, 8Fs and 2–6–0 0–6–2 Beyer Garratts were also encountered along with the occasional Crab or Black 5. Likewise excursions to the north and east could brighten men's days. The popular relief point here was at Landor Street Junction where again a cabin, watering and fire-cleaning facilities were located at the base of an incline, i.e. Camp Hill Bank.

As previously stated, whilst many trains terminated in the Birmingham complex, occasionally they were asked to take them onwards to Burton, Derby, Toton or Leicester, which, with fires and coal reserves past their best, could prove quite challenging, especially the latter route with its more precipitous undulations. These longer runs in effect provided firemen with the opportunity to progressively extend their wings and were very useful in enhancing their practical education over a broad spectrum of railway matters. Whereas the Bank pilot link allowed firemen to intimately learn a four mile stretch, control link work extended this knowledge to several miles in all directions. Indeed, by the end of their 12-month stint they may well have ventured as far south as Bristol and north to Sheffield. Although these adventures would probably be the result of some dire emergency, they at least gave a glimpse of what longer journeys held in store and either whetted eager appetites or caused the 'not so keen' to reconsider their positions.

In order to give the reader some idea with regard to different firing techniques for different classes of locomotives on a variety of duties, it will be interesting to see how our trainee firemen would have coped with a Class 4F running from Washwood Heath to Bromsgrove on a bright sunny evening in mid May. We will assume the train was a Beeston to Gloucester class H mixed freight of 42 vehicles that had been delayed to the extent that their Nottingham crew needed to be relieved so that they could catch a return working. Our new crew were pleased to see that the fire appeared to be quite bright, the coal was of reasonable quality and, although somewhat depleted from the very front of the tender, it was piled generously high towards the middle and still falling down onto the shovelling plate. Out on the goods line there was no opportunity to clean the fire and since the general state of the engine seemed fairly good – 170psi showing on the pressure gauge, the boiler three-quarters full and plenty of water in the tank – our crew had no qualms about proceeding without further ado. Most firemen freshly promoted to Control link work had only limited experience of Class 4F locomotives and having just spent up to a year firing from the left side on freely-steaming Class 3Fs, the previously mentioned differences soon became very apparent, particularly if firemen had not perfected the technique of firing from the other side and still felt awkward doing so. The sudden transition to longer-distance duties with a left-hand drive 4F with a fire somewhat past its prime was, therefore, initially doubly taxing.

However, help was always at hand in the form of advice and sometimes demonstration from their drivers so they were not just left to struggle on their own. The first piece was normally given immediately after taking over: "Keep the back corners and under the door well filled with coal and the water level just in sight at the top of the glass". This would be quickly followed by "Don't fire any coal to the front end unless a hole forms and, whatever you do, don't shut the damper – let her blow off if necessary". It was, of course, now essential to maintain a hot furnace, thereby raising the superheater temperature as much as possible before commencing the 4 mile climb to King's Heath. Also it will be recalled that with no superheater, the familiar 3F boilers rallied very rapidly and were extremely tolerant to indifferent management. Class 4Fs were an entirely different kettle of fish and one had to constantly keep on top of the firing, especially when sustained hard work was called for and particularly so when the grate had already consumed a ton or two of coal.

The initial approach towards the base of Camp Hill Bank at Duddeston Road was at a modest 1:326 and as they chuffed steadily past their former colleagues in the West End Pilot Sidings the driver would give '1 short – 1 short' on the whistle, indicating that a pilot was required. After a slight easing approaching Saltley, the gradient stiffened to 1:200, then to 1:172 but because of normal high traffic density on the down goods line, progress was kept down to little more than walking pace in the hope that signals might clear before being obliged to come to a complete

standstill. By using the blower to maintain an adequate draught of air through the fire bed, a bright fire could be achieved despite their light exhaust blast, and, by judicious use of firedoors, blowing off was prevented. This slow crawl towards Duddeston Road's bottleneck was always a time of uncertainty for the crew because their train could be held up here for anything up to an hour or so. However, if diverted on to the intermediate goods loop that ran parallel to the down goods line, then there was a fair chance of more rapid movement since this loop provided the only access to Saltley MPD. Locomotives were continually arriving at the depot for servicing and any delays upset the whole process. Therefore, it was not until reaching Saltley Station that one's route could be known and what action to take.

We will assume that this time the intermediate line signal cleared and so the fireman would be advised to make sure that both back corners of the firebox and 'under the doors' were kept well filled with fresh coal in order that it would be well burnt through by the time they reached Duddeston Road home signals. Another delay might well occur here also, but it was never likely to be lengthy and consequently the same principal of firing was adhered to – level with the bottom of the firehole at the rear, and so thin that it was virtually forming holes at the front. Immediately faced with a rising gradient of 1:105 and the train already standing on an adverse 1:172, a fair amount of energy was required to set things in motion, even with a banker assisting in the rear. It was therefore normal policy to steadily top up the boiler so as to prevent blowing off until the water level was just about at the top of the gauge glass. After that if still detained, a slight amount of blowing off might be acceptable but, because they were in close proximity to Duddeston Road Signal Box, such practice gave rise to general disapproval.

The four mile climb from Duddeston Road to King's Heath is quite a challenge in as much that the steepest part occurs only a couple of hundred yards or so from the start, just beyond Landor Street Junction, where it passes beneath the Western Division's main line to London. With a relatively cold engine struggling to gain speed from a dead standstill on a severe 1:105 gradient, the rise then increases to 1:62 from Brickyard Crossing to Saint Andrew's Junction where a right-hand curve adds significantly to the train's

drag and it is here that they were most likely to stick. The reasons for this embarrassment are many, although perhaps most numerous is excessive slipping, followed by insufficient approach speed, insufficient tractive power, lack of steam or a combination of all four. As may well be imagined, getting away again on a 1:62 gradient, particularly if the rail is greasy, was not at all easy and usually required one or more extra bankers or even an additional train weighing in at the rear to get things moving again.

Therefore, once the signal came off, firemen sprang into frantic activity, opening the blower and releasing the hand brake as quickly as possible. Two or three shovels of pre-broken small cobbles would be sprayed over any very thin areas at the front of the grate and firedoors initially closed completely so that all the draught available was drawn through the firebars. This fierce blast of 'primary air' quickly raised furnace temperature while at the same time closed firedoors precluded cold 'secondary air' from cooling both firebox and tubes unnecessarily, although once hydrocarbons were being given off in quantity from freshly added coal, secondary air admitted via the firehole was required to complete combustion and reduce smoke emissions. Continuing with these techniques of spraying small amounts of coal over the fire bed on the 'little and often' system, 4Fs could usually be persuaded to generate sufficient steam to get their train to the start of the 1:62 section without dropping much below 175psi. For the short climb to and beyond Saint Andrew's Junction, absolute full power frequently became necessary, therefore boiler water level was often 'mortgaged' in order to ensure this. However, with such a steep rising gradient tilting the leading end upwards, boiler water surged to the rear, giving a very optimistic reading in the gauges, but at least this guaranteed the firebox crown remained well covered and lower than normal water levels could be maintained without fear of dropping a fusible plug.

Beyond Saint Andrew's Signal Box the gradient eased somewhat to 1:85, although not until the whole train had passed this point did the likelihood of stalling recede. Then providing the bank pilot maintained his effort, our 4F driver could reduce power output by one of three means. Most usual was to start an injector in order to replace mortgaged boiler water; this steadily reduced steam pressure, thus lowering somewhat drawbar pull. If boiler water level was satisfactory, then the driver would possibly ease back the regulator or adopt his third option of shortening cut-off. Final choice would, as always, depend on conditions at that time, including speed, load and the locomotive's steaming ability. This steady rise continued following the right-hand curve past Saint Andrew's Junction and up the deep cutting adjacent to Birmingham City's football stadium. Speed usually remained constant on this straighter stretch and, providing the Camp Hill down distant signal remained clear, would continue to do so under the wide A45 road bridge, beyond which Bordesley Junction signal box came into view. Once the Saint Andrew's 'sticking point' had been successfully negotiated, firemen could settle into a steady routine of firing, endeavouring to balance the amount of fuel being burnt in the fierce blast with the quantity of fresh coal applied. With LMS-type firedoors, the favoured technique was to direct broken cobbles over a raised combustion plate as consistently as possible. Ideally, this maintained the fire at a constant level without blanketing off radiant heat with a sudden layer of unburned coal producing large quantities of thick black smoke and lowering furnace temperature.

Unfortunately, with Control link work, both conditions and engine were frequently far from ideal. Relieving the crew of a train originating from some distant part only a short time before tackling 'The Bank' meant that there was little opportunity to discover any deficiencies. Even when these did become apparent, not much could be done about them before setting off unless it was of a major nature sufficiently serious as to warrant failing the locomotive. However, numerous minor tribulations, either individually or collectively caused no end of burdens for the crew. These could include poor fuel in the form of low-grade coal, briquettes or slack, which then led to dirty fires, full ashpans, smokeboxes and blocked tubes. Dirty or clinkered fires were always a possibility even with reasonably good coal, especially if they had been poorly fired or the engine had been travelling in excess of four hours. Sometimes they struggled with the handicap of inadequate preparation; for example, going off shed with a smokebox door drawing air, dirty tubes, defective brick arch or burnt baffle plate. Freight engines were rarely in perfect shape when more

than half way through a journey, but then part of a fireman's training was learning how to deal with a multitude of shortcomings and still make the engine perform adequately to complete the work in hand. Indeed all this added to a crewman's sense of achievement and overall satisfaction in a job well done in spite of endless adversity.

Sometimes there was an inordinate amount of very large lumps of coal on the tender and if relief took place during one of those relatively rare moments of rapid progression on the down goods line approaching Duddeston Road, there would be little time to break up an adequate supply before setting forth. This was particularly pertinent where no tender access doors were fitted and firemen had to climb on top in order to reach the coal supply, thereby exposing themselves to numerous hazards when on the move. Regrettably, most 4Fs were coupled to tenders possessing no such doors and in these circumstances firemen were sometimes obliged to use lumps rather larger than strictly ideal. Even so, these were applied in a well tried method. Firehole doors needed to be wide open, of course, and the shovel handled very briskly, with the largest pieces being placed 'under the door' and in the back corners, while smaller cobbles and fines were delivered down both sides towards the front. When the engine was not steaming too freely, a driver would often assist by opening and shutting the doors in synchronisation with his fireman's swings. This team effort was rendered much easier with LMS-type sliding doors than with the old Midland flap design and was practised to reduce the quantity of cold, secondary air entering the firebox while at the same time blanking off some of the white hot radiation reaching an already overheated fireman's flesh.

Just beyond Bordesley Junction, where the gradient eases from a severe 1:85 to a much more moderate 1:280, a steady increase in speed became apparent as the train progressed over the sweeping viaduct that crossed the multitude of former GWR tracks. Providing firemen were doing a pretty reasonable job at this point, furnace temperatures would have risen to something like 2500–2800°F and therefore the superheater would be beginning to deliver some useful benefits. Assuming that the distant signal for Camp Hill was showing a clear aspect, very little alteration would be made to the regulator opening or cut-off position until approaching the

signal box. The crew then needed to decide whether they required the banking engine through to King's Heath or proceed unassisted. Should everything be going well in terms of speed, boiler pressure, water level and fireman's ability to cope, then most drivers would feel confident to relinquish their dependence on rear-end assistance beyond Camp Hill. However, should any of these requirements be below par, or even if some doubt existed, 4F drivers would not hesitate in whistling for the pilot to continue through to King's Heath Station.

As previously indicated, 4Fs were slow to warm from a cold start and initially struggled on the climb to Bordesley Viaduct, often only maintaining near boiler pressure by the expedience of mortgaging boiler water level. Consequently, by the time they were nearing Camp Hill box, the engine was somewhat 'winded' and tended to rely heavily on the pilot over the subsequent easier mile or so at 1:280 through Brighton Road to the start of the short section of 1:108 that rose up through Moseley Tunnel.

During this period of lighter running, opportunity to replenish the boiler water level was gratefully taken so that the final climb to King's Heath could be accomplished without too much loss of momentum. Beyond King's Heath the road is level for a mile or so, and providing Hazelwell's distant signal was off, 4Fs could be linked up to 35–40% cut-off and speed maintained on a partially open regulator. With merely a modest rising gradient of 1:324 > 301 continuing past Lifford Junction to King's Norton Junction, firemen allowed the fire to run down somewhat, since non-fitted trains were usually turned onto the down goods line that ran parallel to the main from King's Norton to Halesowen Junction, where it changed to become the slow line. It may be recalled that the fast line from Birmingham New Street joins from the right at King's Norton and the four tracks then proceed together as far as Barnt Green where fast and slow lines merge as one. Understandably, passenger trains and fitted freights took precedence over slower freights on this section, so that it is a pretty safe bet that if on the latter, one's progress would be along the goods line. Permissive block was in operation on the goods line from King's Norton to Halesowen Junction and particularly at busy times it was not uncommon for a number of freight trains to be moving at a steady pace to what could be a bottleneck at Halesowen Junction. Should this be the case, the signalman at King's Norton would give a green hand signal followed by a number of fingers raised to indicate how many trains preceded yours. Assuming a green signal was given and an indication that two trains were in the section ahead, our crew would acknowledge this with a whistle and an appreciative wave.

There was no point in hurrying in these circumstances, so the engine was set at little above walking pace up the gentle 1:301, 3 mile rise to the junction. Firemen unfamiliar with the route were advised to just maintain steam pressure with no more than two-thirds showing in the water gauge glass and, since to do this required only a few shovels of coal every now and then, they were not exactly overtaxed and could even enjoy a quick drink of tea and a cigarette if they so desired. By travelling at a slow pace, there was every chance that whatever was preceding them might have departed from Halesowen Junction by the time they arrived at the signals, although this was not always the case. Movement along the goods and slow lines was entirely dependent on suitable gaps on the fast where they were permitted to run only between the swifter passenger and express fitted freights.

On this occasion, one of the freight trains ahead had already departed and they had halted behind the preceding train's brake van merely some 10 minutes before it, too, clanked into motion on what was now the slow line that worked to the absolute block system. At the same steady pace they would move over the vacated 300 yard stretch of line to roll to a stop at the track-circuited signal and there await events. Although the block to Barnt Green was 2½ miles long, all of which still climbed at the same 1:301, once under way again their 4F was allowed to amble steadily along in order to conserve effort and therefore fuel. Despite these tactics, the signals remained stubbornly on at Barnt Green for a further 20 minutes after they had come to a standstill and applied the handbrake. Their train was now near the highest elevation of the line, having climbed 230 feet during the 12 miles since leaving Saltley. However, during the next 2½ miles they were going to descend more than 300 feet, most of which was at nearly 1:37.

During this wait at the signals while a number of faster trains sped past, it would

be pointed out to firemen that when the road cleared they needed to proceed with much greater alacrity than before because the slow and fast lines merged into one here and any undue delays had unwanted repercussions. For that reason it would be wise to build a larger fire in the back of the firebox so that it could be easily spread over the entire grate at a moment's notice. It was also pointed out that any relieving fireman would regard filling the coal space above the shovelling plate as a very friendly act and would doubtless express his gratitude in no uncertain manner; in any case, both tasks were more easily achieved while waiting on a static footplate. When a certain amount of fuel depletion had been reached, it was necessary to work coal forward at regular intervals. Naturally, this was safer to accomplish when not moving, since as stated before, without access doors it required climbing over the tender front and, by means of the coal pick, dragging coal down from the higher mound in the centre. Such actions placed firemen well above cab roof level and therefore exposed them to the risk of contact with bridges and other lineside infrastructure.

The inevitable procession of passenger and fitted traffic rattled past and then, without any warning, the signals cleared and both crew members leapt into activity. Blower hard on, damper fully opened, then the shovel blade vigorously dug several times into the mass of well burned-through fire piled under the firehole so as to project it all over the grate area. Meanwhile, the driver wound his reverser down into full forward gear, applied the steam brake in order to more easily release the handbrake and then, after creating vacuum with the small ejector, eased open his regulator. Once the wheels had made a couple of revolutions and all couplings were taut, our driver closed the cylinder drain cocks and then opened up with some purpose, heading for Blackwell with all possible haste.

Acceleration on the descending 1:291 gradient was somewhat more effortless than usual. However, due regard had to be given to the fact that they had around 500 tons in tow and only the engine brake with which to halt its motion. Of all places where instruction boards existed, Blackwell's notice requesting all loose-coupled trains to stop in order to pin down wagon brakes was possibly adhered to more diligently than any other. To proceed 'over the top' with no brakes at all

pinned down would certainly provide more excitement than any engineman was prepared to accept and might possibly terminate in fatal consequences. However, on this occasion they had to be patient a little longer because, as they approached Blackwell, the signal there indicated that they were to enter the loop so that faster traffic could descend the incline unhindered.

While they were waiting amid the splendid, verdant surroundings, opportunity was taken for a final tidy-up with brush and slacking pipe and to quaff the remainder of their tea. Most young firemen, on first sighting the daunting 1:37 Lickey Incline, underwent a mixture of feelings ranging from the excitement of a new adventure to downright trepidation of the unknown, but no matter how experienced, enginemen always held that dead-straight two-mile drop in very considerable awe. Nowhere on the Midland Division was there such an obvious descent, so it invariably came as a surprise to initiates to be told to start building up the fire a little when the signal that released them from the loop cleared.

It was explained to them that although when joining the main line they would roll down a falling 1:291 gradient to the far end of Blackwell Station, they would quite often need quite a lot of steam to drag their 'braked' train onto the 1:37 part of the incline. Just beyond the platform end, an ancient black hut housed the brakeman who, after consultation with the guard, decided on the appropriate number of wagon brakes to be pinned down in accordance with vehicle types, load being conveyed and prevailing conditions. Years of experience ensured these two men could accurately judge the ratio of braked to non-braked wagons which could be, for example, 1 in 3, but they did not always get it dead right for reasons that were sometimes not in their power to anticipate. As previously mentioned, loose-coupled trains were required to halt at the stop board adjacent to the brakeman's hut, where their brakes were pinned down. Normally, with the guard taking the up side and the brakeman the down or platform side, they would walk back along the train, dropping brake handles off their rests but not pinning them down at this stage. On returning to the locomotive, our driver would be instructed to proceed and, providing the Blackwell starter signal had cleared, the regulator was opened gently and the couplings eased out. The art was for the driver to maintain a steady 2–3 mph so that both brakeman and guard could firmly pin down the brakes on each selected wagon as it rolled slowly past them. If the pace was too great, wagons might be only lightly braked or even missed out altogether. In either case, the train would have inadequate brake power and a runaway situation was likely to occur. On the other hand, insufficient speed would result in the train being dragged to a standstill before it was fully on to the 1:37 section. In this instance, brakes would have to be picked up again and then being on the incline proper, a restart usually resulted in much more rapid acceleration, preventing remaining brakes from being successfully secured; indeed the brake van was sometimes travelling so swiftly by the time it reached the guard, that he was unable to jump on board and operate his brake for the descent of the bank.

The technique demanded a great amount of skill from the driver, who had to play it mainly by feel and instinct, continually juggling the regulator in order to keep speed constant against a varying drag as fresh wagon brakes were being pinned down. Against this was the opposite force of gravity trying to accelerate the train as more of it came onto the steepest part of the incline. In 'greasy rail' conditions, matters were doubly difficult since he also had to combat against the locomotive suddenly slipping; in these circumstances, full use was made of the sanding equipment. It also required a high degree of dexterity from both guard and brakeman who needed to be heavy of hand and light of foot. The efficiency of hand braking mechanisms on many common user wagons was something of a lottery, to say the least, and part of the brakeman's skill lay in being able to detect any deficiency in that respect and applying more pressure accordingly to the brake lever before inserting its locking pin. If all proceeded according to plan, the train began to run more easily as a greater number of wagons came onto the 1:37 section and as gravity commenced to play an increasingly important part in the equation. Consequently, the regulator opening could be progressively reduced to just a breath of steam before being closed altogether. During this sequence the driver would get a 'feel' of his train and this indicated to him the brake power that had been imparted to it as well as what the highest speed might be for a controlled

descent. Needless to say, matters did not always go to plan, for no two trains were ever the same and even if they were, the brakes would not be pinned down with exactly the same force. The weather and rail conditions were always different as indeed were locomotives even of the same class and so no honest driver would guarantee stopping exactly where required with a non-fitted train.

Once it was established that the train was running freely without power on and hand signals had been exchanged with the guard confirming that he was safely in his van, firemen would be asked to apply the tender handbrake as firmly as possible. This was achieved by using the power of the engine steam brake to force brake blocks hard onto wheel tyres so that operation of the handbrake was relatively light until it had run its full travel. Normally, the steam brake handle would be quickly returned to its running position and hopefully train speed would be held fairly constant under the restraint imposed by tender, pinned-down wagon brakes and the brake van. The engine steam brake was therefore held in reserve if possible so as to make slight corrections of speed as the descent progressed. On the Lickey incline there is a certain critical speed with every train, above which it is impossible to regain. With the coefficient of friction being the square of velocity, increases of only one mph increments could make all the difference, so judgement had to be exceptionally precise. Accelerating from 5 to 10mph would then require not twice, but four times the brake power to hold the train in check and, unfortunately, this amount was not always available. Maintaining full boiler pressure helped and this is another reason why firemen were told to ensure a reasonable body of fire on the grate as well as for traction at the top of the bank.

Providing a fair job had been done by brakeman and guard, drivers would only apply their steam brake intermittently for short periods. If, however, through miscalculation wagon braking was inadequate, the driver would soon find himself making increasingly longer applications at shorter intervals until it was left permanently on. If speed continued to increase under full braking, then the train was said to be 'in' since there was little else the crew could do other than enjoy the vista from their elevated position. At night, a rapid descent under full braking was an exceedingly spectacular event since from every brake

block showers of Catherine-wheel-like sparks splashed along the whole length of the locomotive's underframes, filling the cab with the pungent stench of burning oil and metal. Whether day or night, though, it was generally conceded that if the train was not under control by the time it reached the distant signals for Bromsgrove, then a runaway was inevitable. The 1:37 section of Lickey Incline ends at Bromsgrove Station where it eases for a short distance to 1:186 before dropping at 1:105 to the water column, relief cabin and signal box at Bromsgrove South. This undulation posed quite a problem for drivers wishing to stop precisely at that water column. The train had its brakes pinned down to suit a 1:37 gradient and was thus much over-braked for 1:186 or even 1:105.

Consequently, deceleration was rapid, progressively unrelenting and difficult, which made calculations and judgement of all the varying forces extremely complex. If the train's descent had been properly led by the driver's engine brake, then there comes a point near the lower end of the 1:37 incline where he released his brake altogether. This was in order to gain sufficient momentum to carry the heavily-braked train over those undulations so as to stop on target for water. Judging this point accurately, particularly at night, was arguably about the most difficult regular driving feat on the Midland Region.

Beyond Bromsgrove South Signal Box the line continued its downward path at 1:283 until Stoke Works Junction some 3 miles distant, to where, on exceptional occasions a few runaway trains have been recorded as travelling before coming to a halt. However, it was far more usual for runaways to only overshoot the water column by between half and a couple of train lengths. Most frustrating, though, was to run past by merely two or three wagons, because with so many brakes pinned down, it was quite impossible to set back even this far on a rising gradient until they had been picked up again. One of the unpredictable causes of such happenings was when on the 'undulations' it became obvious that the train would stop some good way short. The normal practice to overcome this deficiency was to open the regulator and start dragging the train and often this would result in a satisfactory outcome. Unfortunately, if the guard spotted this action, he would try and assist by releasing his brake, but regrettably this frequently caused all the driver's care-

EX MID. RLY. M CLASS BUILT NEILSON 1896/7.
H BOILERED 1906. REBUILT SATURATED BELPAIRE 1942.
W/DRAWN 1959. NOTTINGHAM 1927, GLOUCESTER 1935,
AND 1948.

The change in gradient at the bottom of the Lickey Incline can be seen in this 12th July 1939 view of Class 3F No. 3506 at the head of a mineral train running along the platform line prior to coming to a stand at Bromsgrove South signal box where the locomotive would take on water, the wagon brakes would be released and maybe there would have been a change of engine crew and guard.

H. C. CASSERLEY

ful calculations to become suddenly undone. The raft of wagons being restrained by his brake van until that moment ran free, and their collective weight delivered a hefty push from the rear, usually at the precise moment the engine's tender was being lined up to the water column. As previously indicated, being pushed past the column by only two wagon lengths was nearly as time-wasting as running past a whole train length inasmuch that all wagon brakes had to be picked up before it was possible to set back for water. In order to expedite this procedure, the fireman would set off down one side using his coal pick handle as a brake stick while the guard took the other; after all, if being relieved at Bromsgrove, it was the crew's meal time that was being wasted. For these unpredictable reasons which drivers encountered as they gained experience, they generally settled for stopping, if at all possible, slightly short of the column. The engine could then be easily uncoupled, run forward, watered and returned to its train by the time the guard had lifted the pinned-down brakes.

We will assume our novice fireman's first descent was a perfectly normal, well-led one with no unexpected incidents and his driver brought the engine to a halt a few wagon lengths short of the column in the manner described above. While watering, the driver established that they were being relieved and that they would be required to work a train back to Saltley, but they still had plenty of time to enjoy their meal break.

In the next article we will see how firemen coped with their first experience of ascending the formidable Lickey Incline with a freight train.

This article will follow the Lickey Incline article, which will be in four parts. Editor

Bromsgrove South signal box with the water crane where down trains were due to come to a stand. COLLECTION R. S. CARPENTER

Taken in 1939, this photograph shows a tail lamp on a D1860 3rd Corridor No. 1325 which was branded as 'A' stock. Unfortunately, I have never found the official description of what constituted 'A' stock.

NATIONAL RAILWAY MUSEUM (DY25465)

LMS HEAD, SIDE AND TAIL LAMPS

by BOB ESSERY

IF a railwayman from the steam era was asked which was the most important light on the railway, I would expect the reply to be the tail lamp. When I started to write this article, I began by looking at the oldest railway rulebook in my collection in order to see what the early Victorian railwaymen had to say about tail lamps.

Midland Railway Rules and Regulations
For the Guidance
of the
OFFICERS AND MEN
IN THE SERVICE OF
THE COMPANY.
NOVEMBER, 1851

This rulebook was published some seven and a half years after the formation of the Company, so we are not too far away from the dawn of the railway age and certainly during the early formative years of the steam railway. I also have a copy of the January 1855 Rules and Regulations, which, as far as these rules are concerned, are identical. Four rules are worth quoting in full, beginning with the section headed 'Regulations to be observed by GUARDS'. This stated: '43. – No Guard shall allow his Train to travel on the Line after sunset, unless there shall be attached thereto, and lighted, a Red Tail Lamp and two Red Side Lamps.' Another rule in the guard's section said: '56. – When a Train has a Red Board or Flag, or Red Tail Lamp affixed the rear of it, the Guard is to see that such Signal is removed at the proper Station, and report to the Station-Master that a Special Train is coming.'

There were also one rule in the section of the book described as 'Regulations to be observed by Enginemen & Firemen that is relevant to the subject': '84. – No Engine without a Train shall pass along the Line after sunset, unless a Lighted Red Tail Lamp shall be affixed at the back thereof.' Although the rule is not clear about what happened during daylight hours, I assume that the lamp was carried on the appropriate lamp holder.

From these rules it is possible to see that almost from the earliest days of the railway a red tail lamp and two sidelights were required, but the need for a locomotive headlamp came later. Although I have not been able to establish a precise date, it

TAIL LAMPS AND SIDE LIGHTS ON TRAINS.

Referring to Rule 127 in the Book of Rules and Regulations; except where instructions are issued to the contrary, all freight, etc., trains must carry side lights on the rear brake van, and passenger and empty coaching stock trains must carry side lights on the brake vehicle in which the rear guard is riding, as follows:—

(A) On main lines where there are only two lines and on single lines ... ... One red tail light and two red side lights.

(B) On main lines where there are three or four lines:—

   (i) On the fast line ... ... One red tail light and two red side lights.

   (ii) On the slow, goods or loop lines... One red side light on the side of the van furthest away from fast line, one white side light on the side of the van nearest the fast line, and one red tail light (See note).

(C) On goods or loop lines adjoining four main lines ... ... One red tail light only. Side lamps must be removed when the train has passed into the loop.

NOTE.—Certain brake vans are provided with a side lamp which, when turned to show a white light to the rear, shows a red light to the front. In such cases the instructions in paragraph (B) (ii) will not apply, and the side lamp instead of being turned must be removed.

A signalman will not be required to send the "Tail light out, tail lamp in wrong position or improper side light exhibited" signal when a train passes his box with the side light removed as directed.

Rail motors and motor trains, also electric trains, do not carry side lights.

Side lamps must be carried on the rear brake van of all freight, mineral and empty wagon trains (local trips excepted) during the day as well as by night.

(Refer to Sectional Appendices for portions of the line upon which side lamps are not carried.)

This view of the rear of an ex-L&Y goods brake van, photographed at Stratford-on-Avon in 1952, shows the arrangement of the three lamps on the rear of a goods brake van. In order to change the shade, the guard came onto the verandah, but on some brake vans the colour of the lamp was changed from inside the van. I recall that some guards said the they disliked this arrangement because of the smell of the paraffin which could not be avoided when the lamp was lit.

COLLECTION
R. J. ESSERY

seems likely it would be when the change from Time Interval to the Block System began and the need to identify oncoming trains became more important. In my article 'An introduction to LMS traffic' (*LMS Journal* No. 3, page 5), I covered the question of locomotive headlamp codes, so I do not intend to repeat what was said, other than to include the drawing of the locomotive headlamps; in this article I will only consider tail and side lamps and their use in service during the LMS period.★

We begin by referring to this extract taken from the 1931 General Appendix to the Working Time Tables dated January 1st 1931 Until Further Notice. There can be no doubt about what is required – one tail light and two side lights on all goods and passenger trains. Note the requirements for showing a white sidelight when the train was not running on the fast line. This rule continued for all freight trains into the British Railways era when the rule for 'fully fitted' freight trains was changed and side lights were not required; only a tail lamp was carried. Before we consider the 1937 General Appendix, I

TAIL LAMPS AND SIDE LIGHTS ON TRAINS.

Referring to Rule 120; the following instructions apply to trains working over the L.M.S. Railway:—

Mixed trains with a freight train guard's brake van in rear must carry side lamps as laid down for freight trains.

Except where instructions are issued to the contrary, all freight trains or engines with freight train guard's brake van or vans must carry side lights on the rear brake van as follows:—

(A) On main lines where there are only
two lines and on single lines......... One red tail light and two red side lights.

(B) On main lines where there are
three or four running lines:—

    (i.) On the fast line............... One red tail light and two red side lights.

    (ii.) On the slow, goods, or loop
lines..................................... One red side light on the side of the van furthest away from the fast line; one white side light on the side of the van nearest the fast line, and one red tail light. (*see Note*).

(C) On goods or loop lines adjoining
four main lines............................... One red tail light only. Side lamps must be removed when the train has passed into the loop.

Note.—Certain brake vans are provided with side lamps which cannot be turned, or which, when turned to show a white light to the rear, show a red light to the front. In these cases the instructions in paragraph (B) (ii.) will not apply, and the side lamp instead of being turned must be removed. A signalman will not be required to send the "Tail or side light out, or improper side light exhibited" signal when a train passes his box with side light removed as directed.

Where side lights are shown to be carried the side lamps must, except in the case of local trips, be carried on the rear brake van during daylight as well as during darkness.

The instructions in clause (a) of Rule 120 respecting the carrying, cleaning, trimming, and lighting of tail lamps also apply to light engines.

Tail lamps on passenger trains.—The guard, or rear guard where there is more than one, must see that the tail lamp is properly fixed before signalling the train away. This will not, however, relieve from responsibility any of the platform staff who should affix tail lamps.

Station Masters and inspectors must pay special attention when vehicles are attached or detached, and see that the tail lamp is in its proper position.

A clean trimmed tail lamp must be carried inside the rear van of all trains provided with gas tail lamps, and in each portion where there is more than one van provided with gas tail lamps.

L.N.E. Railway (G.E. Section) coaching stock brake vans with fitted tail lamps.— When one of these brake vans is the rear vehicle on a train, the fixed tail lamp must not be used and an ordinary oil tail lamp must be carried both by day and by night.

Extinguishing lights in side and tail lamps.—At the completion of the train journey and after the train is shunted into a siding clear of the running lines, the guard, before leaving the train, must, unless instructions are issued to the contrary, extinguish the lights in the side and tail lamps.

Freight, etc., trains, assisted in rear——Tail and side lamps.

Referring to Rule 133; when a freight train is assisted in rear by an engine or by an engine propelling one or two brake vans, the guard of the freight train must remove his tail lamp. When the train is assisted by an engine drawing one or two brake vans, the guard of the freight train must, in addition to removing the tail lamp, remove his side lamps, and side lamps must be carried on the rearmost brake van attached to the assisting engine.

★The details given in the 1937 General Appendix also shown at page 77 of *LMS Journal* No. 15.

should explain the apparent anomaly about rule 127. This is not rule 127 in the LMS rule book; the first LMS Rule Book was not published until 1st January 1933. Until that date, the Railway Clearing House Standard Rules, with such additions or amendments that the various companies made, applied. However, the essential detail of that rule is reproduced in the General Appendix.

When we compare the 1931 extract to the 1937 General Appendix we can see that there is no reference to side lamps on passenger trains in the later edition. Unfortunately, I am unable to say when it ceased to be a requirement, and if any reader can help I would be most grateful. I can only assume that during the early 1930s it was realised there could be a saving to the railway company if two lights could be dispensed with on all passenger trains. The 1937 extract to the General Appendix refers to Rule 120 and, since this is an LMS rule, I have included an extract from the Company's rule book to show what was said. I have also included rules 119, 121 (this is dealt with in the General Appendix) 122, 123 and 124, which all are relevant to the subject.

This picture shows the brake end of a D1693 3rd Class Vestibule Brake No. 638, which became No. 9835 after 1933. Built at Wolverton in 1927, the small side light can be seen above the side ducket. What is unclear is whether the sidelights were illuminated by paraffin or electricity. I expect that LMS-built coaches used electricity and the Midland vehicles burned paraffin.
NATIONAL RAILWAY MUSEUM

HEAD, TAIL AND SIDE LAMPS.

119. Each engine, or leading engine when two or more engines are coupled together, and each rail motor, motor train, or electric train, must carry the prescribed head lamps, discs, or indicators, and destination boards where provided. The head lamps and indicators must be alight after sunset and during fog or falling snow, and where otherwise provided. *Distinctive head lamps, discs, &c.*

120. (a) Each train when on any running line must always have a tail lamp, properly cleaned and trimmed, attached to the rear of the last vehicle, and this lamp will furnish evidence to the Signalman and others that the train is complete. After sunset, or during fog or falling snow, or when the block apparatus has failed in a section where there is a tunnel, or where otherwise provided, the tail lamp must be alight and show a red light and, except in the case of passenger and other trains composed of coaching stock, and light engines, two red side lights must also be carried. *Tail lamp to indicate last vehicle.*

(b) The Guard, if there be only one, or rear Guard if there be more than one, must see that the tail lamps, and side lamps where provided, are kept properly burning when necessary. *Guard to see that tail and side lamps are burning.*

121. Where trains travel in the same direction on parallel lines, special regulations for head, side and tail lamps will be issued as necessary. *Head, side and tail lamps—parallel lines.*

122. (a) An engine without a train must, when on any running line, always carry a tail lamp in the rear. *Engine tail lamp.*

(b) When two or more engines are run coupled together without a train, the last engine only must have a tail lamp attached.

(c) An engine or engines drawing a train must not carry any lamp in the rear.

(d) An engine assisting a train in the rear must have a tail lamp attached; when more than one engine assists, the tail lamp must be carried on the rearmost engine only.

123. Engines employed exclusively in shunting at station yards and sidings must, after sunset or during fog or falling snow, carry head and tail lamps both showing a red light or such other light as may be prescribed. *Shunting engines*

124. (a) An additional tail lamp or a red board or a red flag by day, or an additional red tail light by night, carried on the last vehicle of a train or on any engine, indicates that a special train is to follow, of which previous printed or written notice has not been given. Signalmen and others concerned must keep a look out for such indication. *Special trains run without notice.*

(b) The Station Master at the starting point of any such special train must, when practicable, take care that the additional tail signal is affixed on the last vehicle of the preceding train and the Guard must see that the additional tail signal is removed when no longer required.

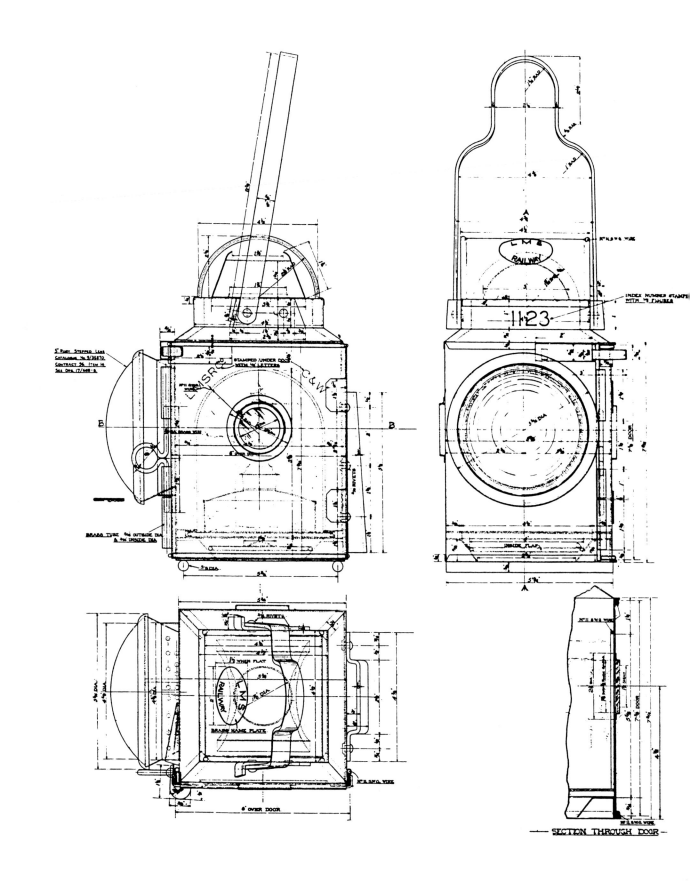

SECTION THROUGH DOOR

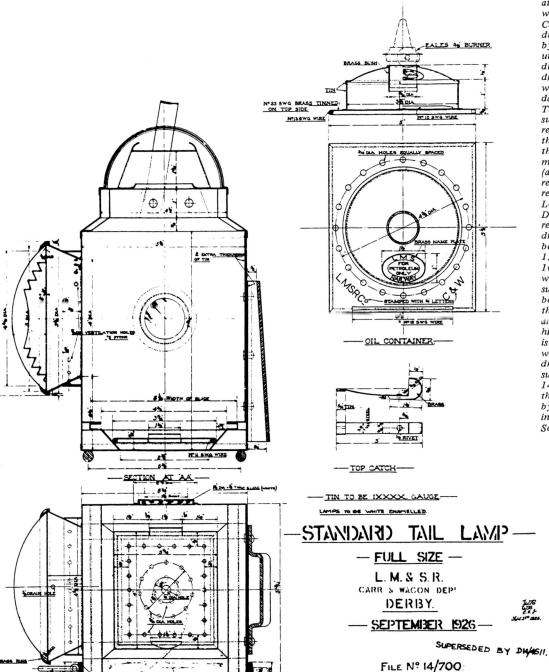

EALES ⅜ BURNER

BRASS BUSH

TIN

Nº 23 SWG BRASS TINNED ON TOP SIDE

Nº 13 SWG WIRE

Nº 12 SWG WIRE

⅜ DIA HOLES EQUALLY SPACED

BRASS NAME PLATE

LMS Rº

L M S FOR PETROLEUM ONLY RAILWAY

C & W

STAMPED WITH 4 LETTERS

Nº 10 SWG WIRE

— OIL CONTAINER —

½ TIN

BRASS

1/16 RIVET

— TOP CATCH —

2 EXTRA THICKNESS OF TIN

VENTILATION HOLES ½ PITCH

WIDTH OF SLIDE

Nº 11 SWG WIRE

— SECTION AT 'AA' —

TIME GLASS (WHITE)

DRAIN HOLE

BRASS RING

Nº 11 SWG WIRE

— SECTIONAL PLAN AT 'BB' —

— TIN TO BE IXXXX. GAUGE. —

LAMPS TO BE WHITE ENAMELLED.

STANDARD TAIL LAMP —

— FULL SIZE —

L. M. & S. R.
CARR & WAGON DEPT
DERBY.

— SEPTEMBER 1926 —

SUPERSEDED BY D14/4511.

FILE Nº 14/700.

This drawing provides a good example of how research can also be frustrating. During the years that Fred James and I sorted and recorded the Derby locomotive drawings at the NRM, York, we were also aware that the Carriage and Wagon drawings were to be listed by others. Unfortunately, unlike the locomotive drawings, the Derby C&W drawing register ceases with drawing No. 6701 dated 21st January 1927. The whereabouts, if it has survived, of the later register is not known to the writer or the staff at the NRM. To complicate matters further, many (all?) drawings were renumbered. Note the reference File No. 14/700. Looking at my copy of the Derby C&W drawing register, the page covering drawings 6009-6024 have been renumbered into the 13/xx, 14/xx, 15/xx and 16/xx series. In discussions with Philip Millard, he suggested this may have been related to the size of the original drawing and I am inclined to agree with him. What is also unknown is what drawing D14/4511 was on the date it was drawn and why it superseded 6614, now 14/700. What I can say is that this drawing was made by W. Rhodes and the date in the register is 16th September 1926.

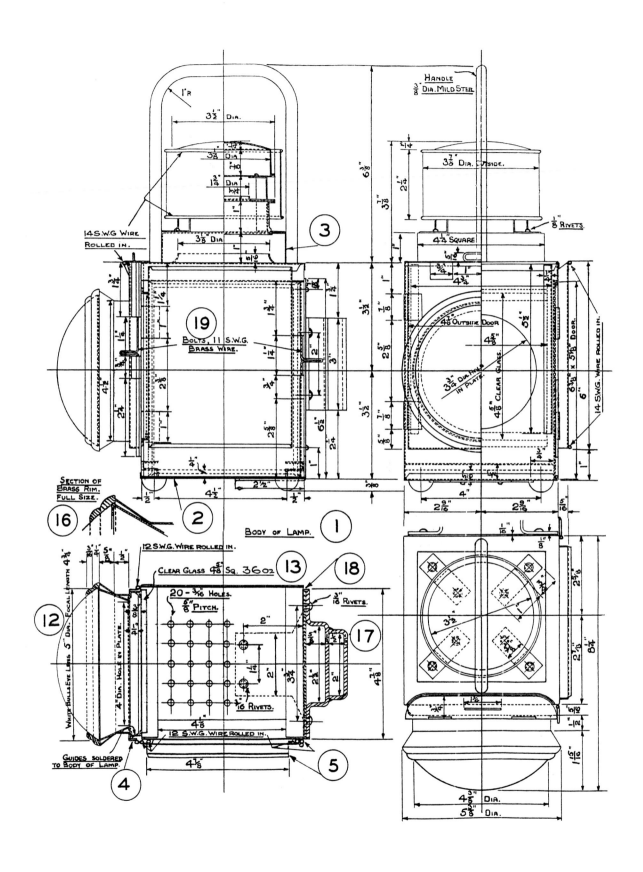

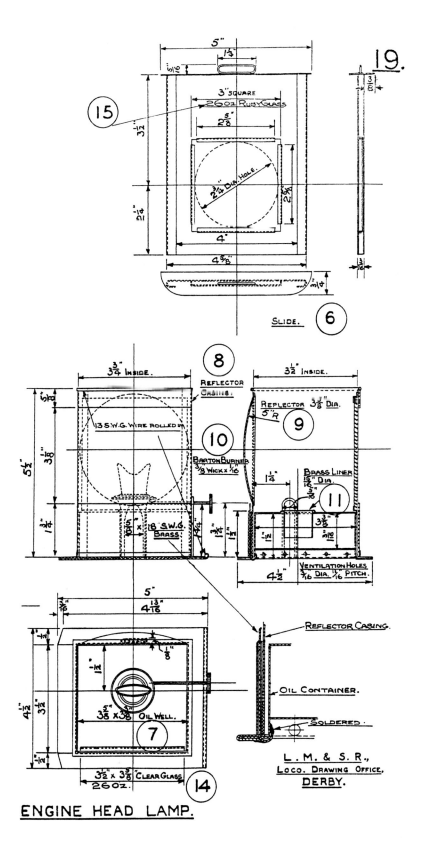

19.

SLIDE. ⑥

ENGINE HEAD LAMP.

L. M. & S. R.,
LOCO. DRAWING OFFICE,
DERBY.

This drawing has been in my collection for many years but, unlike the other drawings that have been reproduced in this article, there is no drawing number or date shown. Note that it is attributed to the Loco Drawing Office Derby, whereas the drawings on pages 34, 35 and 38, 39 are Carriage & Wagon Department, Derby drawings.

According to the Derby C&W Department drawing register, this drawing was made by W. Rhodes and the date in the drawing register is 28th October 1926. However, in between drawing 6614 and 6632 he also made drawing 6620, described in the register as 'Standard Staff Van for Breakdown Trains'.

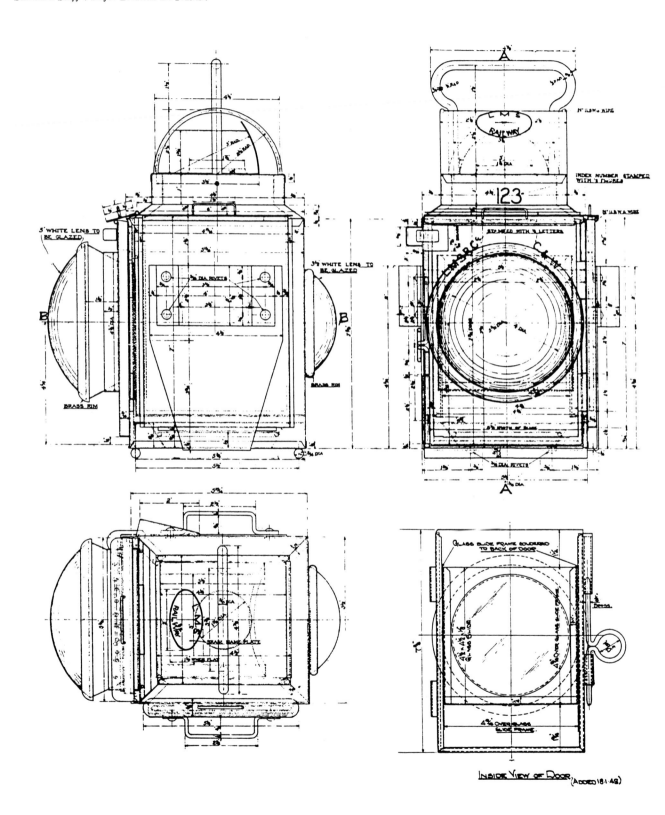

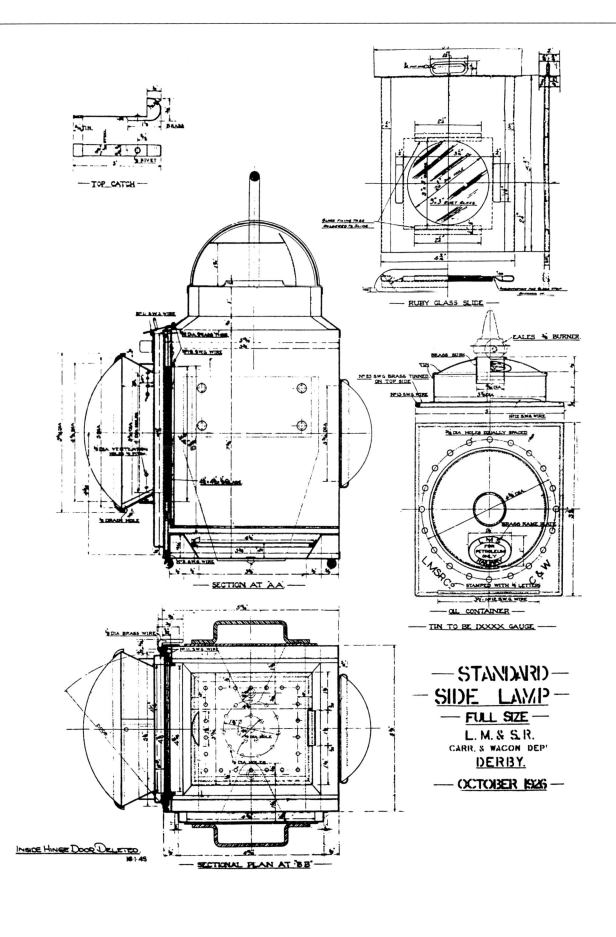

— TOP CATCH —

— RUBY GLASS SLIDE —

— SECTION AT 'AA' —

OIL CONTAINER

TIN TO BE IXXXX GAUGE

— SECTIONAL PLAN AT 'BB' —

INSIDE HINGE DOOR DELETED.
16·1·49

— STANDARD —
SIDE LAMP
— FULL SIZE —
L. M. & S. R.
CARR. & WAGON DEP'
DERBY.
— OCTOBER 1926 —

One of the enduring memories of my footplate years was when we were running on the up main line approaching King's Norton. At this point the up goods line is parallel to the main line and it was not uncommon for there to be anything up to five goods trains nose-to-tail waiting for a path to run over the Camp Hill line to Washwood Heath or Water Orton. During the hours of darkness, the goods guard would change the side light in his brake van that was next to the main line from red to white when his train ran onto the goods line; this was done by removing the red shade, but sometimes the guard, comfortable in his warm, cosy brake van, would fall asleep before the change was made. The first time I saw 'three reds' in front of my engine I thought there was a train in front of us on the main line, but my driver reassured me and said, 'The guard's asleep and hasn't removed the red shade, I'll wake him up'. As we passed the brake van he threw a piece of coal at the side of it and later I learned it was common practice for enginemen to wake up the guard if he had not removed the red shade.

The late David Jenkinson and I began to research the subject of LMS and Midland coaching stock in 1964 and the final volume was published in 2000. At the time, I recall saying to David, I wonder if there is anything we have missed? Although we decided that we had made a comprehensive study of the subject, it is clear that we had overlooked the question of sidelights on coaches. Therefore, in a way, this article is a postscript to our previous titles on the subject.

This picture, taken at Saltley in 1934, shows a gas-lit ex-Midland Railway D503 3rd Brake No. 97, which was later renumbered 27746. When photographed, it was part of a set of close-coupled six-wheel carriages. Note the shape of the sidelight, which differs from the LMS-built vehicle and appears to have been lit by paraffin.
R. E. LACY

FURTHER INFORMATION ON LMS LOCOMOTIVE PROFILES From the series editor, DAVID HUNT

ONCE again, it is gratifying to report that amendments and additions to our books continue to come in. A couple of contributors have started off by writing, 'I hope you don't mind me pointing out,' or similar, to which my response is, 'Not at all; in fact, we welcome it unreservedly'. As I have stated before, we are not smug enough to imagine that we know everything about the subject of LMS locomotives, nor that we are incapable of making mistakes – even some very silly ones! Part of the ethos of the books is to publish what we can and hope that our efforts bring out into the open as much information as possible from the treasury that resides with the readership. In short, keep it coming so that as many folk as possible can benefit from your knowledge. For those readers who are not aware of the change in the on-line situation, I can be contacted via the LMS Society website at *www.lmssociety.org.uk* as well as email at *dvhunt@aol.com* and by post via Wild Swan Publications. A few readers have noticed that we produce the titles in collaboration with the National Railway Museum and have written to the research staff there with comments. I would ask you not to do that as they have no involvement with the preparation of the books and all such correspondence is just forwarded to me via the publisher, which only results in delay.

LMS Locomotive Profile No. 1 – The rebuilt 'Royal Scots'
On page 41 we stated that the only engine fitted with roller bearings on the inside big end was 46128. Reader Tony Gillett was MIC secretary at Lostock Hall shed when it closed and has a copy of a memo from the Accrington District Motive Power Superintendent that shows Nos. 46114,

46120, 46125, 46128, 46129, 46134, 46136, 46163 and 46169 were so fitted.

Tony Gillett also tells me that the cab roof had a transverse joint that dripped water down backs of footplatemen's necks and was a constant source of complaint. It was never altered, though, as the rear of the cab roof had to be removable for access to the hind lifting points.

LMS Locomotive Profile No. 4 – The 'Princess Royal' Pacifics

Ex-fireman and driver E. Padfield, who worked at Camden shed and knew the Class well, points out that the firehole door flap is not shown in the drawing on page 67. From other queries raised by Mr. Padfield, it is apparent that we should make it clear that this drawing shows Nos. 6203–6212 as built, later alterations being described in the text.

LMS Locomotive Profile No. 6 – The Mixed Traffic Class 5s Part 2

Following a query by Kevin Smith, we looked again at the question of roller bearings on tenders and realised that we made a mistake on page 77 by stating that they were made by Timken. In fact, they were made by whichever company produced the locomotive bearings, so the tenders coupled to engines 44678–44687 when built had SKF examples.

John Taylor wrote, 'I was a youngster in the early 1950s with an avid interest in railways, any spare moments were spent in the vicinity of Edge Hill shed and the gridiron. In addition to the 'Black 5s' painted green I remember that one in the 447xx series was painted blue in the same shade as was applied to 8P locos. I have never seen mention of this in print but am sure it was not a figment of childish imagination'. Can any other reader remember a blue Class 5? I was also a youngster living in the Edge Hill area in the 1950s and a frequent visitor to the shed (having an uncle who worked there) but have to admit that I don't recall one.

Photographic Supplement to LMS Locomotive Profile No. 6 – The Mixed Traffic Class 5s Part 2

Driver E. Padfield has again contributed and taken us to task for stating in several captions that the lever alongside the right-hand side of the firebox was connected with the rocking firegrate. The offending captions are on page 10 showing 44999, page 28 showing 44767, page 39 showing 44784, page 52 showing 44680 and page 60 showing 44661. This is a classic case of receiving material from a secondary source and not checking it properly, which is another lesson re-learned. The lever was, in fact, what was known to firemen and drivers as a scale cock lever and operated the blowdown valve.

LMS Locomotive Profile No. 7 – The Mixed Traffic Class 5s – Caprotti valve gear

Several readers have been surprised to find that the drawing on the front cover is fairly obviously an 8F. This was a mistake by the printers, who used the wrong one when setting up the cover template.

John Edgington tells me that the picture on page 25 was taken at Birmingham New St. between platforms 7 & 8.

Roller bearing axleboxes

This point pertains to several of our works and refers to the statements we have made concerning roller bearing axleboxes along the lines of:

'The boxes were originally oil filled but developed problems through condensation emulsifying the oil and leading to corrosion, so drainage was improved and starting in about 1950 they were altered to grease lubrication. To indicate the type fitted, the characteristic circular covers on the roller bearing boxes were painted plain yellow if oil filled and yellow with red horizontal stripes if grease lubricated.'

Regular contributor Dennis Monk, who was a Mechanical Inspector at Derby, has contacted me to say that this is not quite true. Although there were problems with water contamination and drainage had to be improved, this was not the primary reason for changing to grease lubrication. When the early BR diesels appeared, they had Timken boxes that were oil filled and had to be dipped every week to check the oil level, which was inconvenient as the locomotives could be anywhere on the system when the check became due. Since the subject of roller bearing boxes on diesels was Dennis's responsibility and SKF boxes were grease filled, requiring no dipping, he asked Timken if their boxes could also use grease. Eventually they agreed and a start was made converting the Timken boxes in the late 1950s. So that grease-filled boxes could be easily distinguished, even when locomotives were standing close together in gloomy sheds, Dennis suggested painting their end covers yellow and this was adopted. The red stripes were a later addition and whilst Dennis thinks that they were something to do with a different type of grease, by then he wasn't involved with them any more and can't be sure. If any other reader can add to this subject, I would be grateful for their input.

As usual, I would like to offer my thanks to all those who have contributed. Without these people, the story will remain incomplete to the detriment of all. Finally, many readers have been asking me about our future plans. At the time of writing the publication of *LMS Locomotive Profile No. 10* on the 4Fs (both Midland and LMS) is imminent with a photographic supplement at an advanced stage. Two more titles in preparation concern the 'Coronation' Class Pacifics and the 'Twin Motor' diesel shunters, the former also being accompanied by a photographic supplement.

One of my favourite locomotives is the Class 4 0–6–0 and to provide readers with a flavour of what is to come I offer this view of No. 4270 in what I would describe as 'usual condition'. Notwithstanding various authors' critical comments about the class, once I had mastered their 'quirks', I enjoyed firing them, in particular on the Birmingham to Bristol express freight trains.
(Editor)

No. 16911, a Drummond engine, was transferred on loan from Hurlford to Workington in April 1934 and this was made permanent in the September. Nonetheless, it moved further south to Barrow almost immediately and it is here seen inside the shed in 1935. In January 1937 it was transferred to Upperby where it remained until recalled to Hurlford in January 1942.
COLLECTION
R. J. ESSERY

The transfer dates of eight of the South West tanks to Toton in the early thirties seem mostly to be lost in the mists of time. However, in 16904's case, it went first to Sheffield before going to Toton where this c.1936 photograph is believed to have been taken. In February 1937 it was sold out of service to Ashington Coal Co., Northumberland, where it was joined four months later by Ayr's 16908. At the colliery they became Nos. 1 and 2 and lasted until March 1953 and June 1956 respectively.
A. G. ELLIS

IN A FOREIGN FIELD

by KEITH MILES

No. 16926 left Ardrossan for Stourton to work the adjacent sidings in December 1934 but within a couple of months or so it was transferred to Leeds, only to return to Stourton in October 1939. Parked against open-cab 0–6–0T 1813, it is seen at the end of one of the shed's turntable roads. No. 1813 lasted until May 1954 at Hasland but 16926 returned to Scotland in May 1942 where it was eventually withdrawn in December 1945.
COLLECTION V. R. ANDERSON

DURING my time as an Engineering Apprentice at St. Rollox I was fortunate to see representatives of the two surviving classes of the Glasgow & South Western locomotive fleet, regretfully none of them in steam. The last of the so-called 'Austrian Goods' 2–6–0s stationed at Corkerhill were little used, variously described by observers as 'out of use' or 'derelict', and the few surviving 0–6–2Ts were, by then, stationed at the southern end of the Northern Division at Kingmoor. I was only able to come across them as lifeless hulks in the works 'Dump' as they passed through on their way to oblivion. Subsequently, however, I discovered that, in an earlier life, almost half of the original twenty-eight tank engines had once worked even further south, deep into the Midland Division where some of them perished, to remain forever in a foreign field. But first a word about their origins …

The class was introduced by Peter Drummond in 1915 for work in the Ayrshire coalfield which, until then, had been handled by venerable six-coupled tender engines. Six were delivered initially, supplemented by another dozen in 1917. Construction had commenced on an additional ten when PD, as he was known among enginemen, died in office and his successor, R. H. Whitelegg, was able to make some adjustments to the design before their delivery in 1919. Mainly minor in character, the most visible modifications were increased capacity water tanks and a curved outline to the cab cutouts identical to that on his LT&SR 0–6–2Ts. So far as the enginemen were concerned, the most satisfactory modification was the move back to right-hand drive.

In the mid-thirties, for some, as yet, unfathomed reason, fifteen of the engines were transferred to English sheds; two into the nearest Western Division districts and the remainder into the heart of the

Midland Division, as indicated by the accompanying table. I've been unable to ascertain the precise dates for some of the moves but most quoted are as published in contemporary issues of the RCTS *Railway Observer*. It will be noted that eight ended up at Toton where they were engaged in shunting and freight duties. By a curious coincidence, during the same period they were joined in this endeavour by ten of the Midland 'flatiron' 0–6–4 passenger tanks, all this before mechanisation of Toton down yard which took place in 1938/9.

The Midland engines had led a not untroubled life since their introduction in 1907 but a couple of accidents in the spring of 1935 seemed to bring about a watershed in their fortunes and by late summer that year no less than twenty of them were in store; one at Coalville, two at Leicester, four each at Derby and Bournville and nine at Saltley. Nevertheless, in the autumn a mixed bag of six stored and active engines, 2002/9/10/20/ 23/24, were sent to Toton, followed by 2008/13/25/32 up to February 1936. 'But as the class as a whole was something of an assembly of lame ducks' (E. S. Cox, *Locomotive Panorama*, Ian Allan 1965), general withdrawal of the class commenced almost immediately, the last to go being one of the Toton engines, 2032, in May 1938.

TABLE

Table of the G&SWR 0–6–2Ts moves into and around England so far as they can be ascertained. A certain amount of licence has been used in the test in the phrase 'remain forever in a foreign field' since it's known that at least 16906 and 16912 returned to Scotland for scrapping.

As for the Sou'West engines, the number was gradually whittled away, mostly by withdrawals, until the remaining half-dozen were recalled back home to Hurlford in January 1942. Perhaps I should also mention that the nine Caley 'Jumbos' transferred into the Leeds District at the outbreak of war were returned to the Northern Division at the same time. However, the two 0–6–2Ts which are of particular interest insofar as this account is concerned, are 16913 and 16920. These were transferred to Wellingborough in 1937 and, fortunately, first-hand accounts of their activities have been left by George Bushell in his *LMS Footplate Memories* and *LMS Locos from the Footplate* both published by Bradford Barton.

It seems that the job on which they were usually employed was the Henlow Sidings shunt. Not to be confused with Henlow on the Bedford–Hitchin line, Henlow Sidings was a fan of dead-end roads on an embankment at the north-east corner of Neilson's Sidings. Situated on the up side, just over a mile north of Wellingborough, Neilson's dealt mainly with loaded coal traffic from the Erewash Valley which it separated for forward working to stations on the LNW line to Northampton, Bedford, Luton, St. Albans, various depots in the London area and on to the Southern Railway. The Henlow group of sidings was used to sort out wagons for local destinations and the job was booked in the Old Man's Link.

Most sheds had a link of this nature to accommodate drivers of advanced age who wished to relinquish the rigours and often long hours of main-line work. At Rowsley, for example, the actual top link was the London Link which involved several weeks of lodging turns whereas the Old Man's Link encompassed local shunts and trip workings plus the two Derby passenger services. Movement from one link to the other was voluntary rather than the normal promotional advancement. It was also common practice at many sheds to book passed firemen into that link so that they were readily available for filling any vacant or special driving turns. In that eventuality, passed cleaners got the opportunity of stepping up onto the footplate. George Bushell who, as a passed fireman, was a contemporary of mine at Willesden in 1949, was then a passed cleaner at Wellingborough and benefited from this arrangement.

Now it seems that Henlow Sidings, because of the location, was one of the bleakest places in the area during winter. Nevertheless, George found that, although the Sou'West tanks seemed large and cumbersome compared with the standard 0–6–0Ts, the cab was roomy and comfortable, having a generous seat box on the fireman's side. With a piece of tarpaulin rigged up to keep out the worst of the east wind it could be 'almost cosy.' Furthermore, the engines were strong and well suited to their allotted task of loose-shunt-

G&SWR 0–6–2Ts IN ENGLAND

Number	1933	*Subsequent allocations to withdrawal or return to Scotland*			
16904	Ardrossan	Sheffield	Toton	2/37 WDN and sold to Ashington Coal Co.	
16905	Ardrossan			10/37 Workington	1/42 Hurlford
16906	Ardrossan	Toton		6/38 WDN	
16907	Ayr	Toton		4/37 Blair Atholl	
16911	Hurlford	9/34 Workington	Barrow	1/37 Upperby	1/42 Hurlford
16912	Ardrossan	Toton		6/38 WDN	
16913	Hurlford			2/37 Wellingborough	1/38 WDN
16919	Ardrossan	12/34 Carlton	2/35 Leeds	11/37 WDN	
16920	Ardrossan	Toton		9/37 Wellingborough	1/42 Hurlford
16921	Ayr	12/34 Toton	6/35 Stourton	Leeds	1/42 Hurlford
16922	Ayr	6/35 Stourton	10/35 Toton	5/40 Hasland	1/42 Hurlford
16923	Ayr	12/34 Leeds	Toton	1/38 WDN	
16924	Ayr	12/34 Stourton	2/35 Leeds	5/36 WDN	
16925	Ayr	12/34 Stourton		3/36 WDN	
16926	Ardrossan	12/34 Stourton	2/35 Leeds	10/39 Stourton	1/42 Hurlford

Ayr's No. 16907 went to Toton in the early thirties but was transferred to Perth in April 1937 to work at the sub-shed of Blair Atholl where it joined 16902, transferred from Hurlford in August 1935. These Whitelegg engines were used as bankers up the fearsome seventeen-mile climb at mostly 1 in 70 to Druimuachdar, 1,484 feet above sea level, a task previously undertaken by Peter Drummond's 0–6–4Ts built for the Highland Railway. Here No. 16902 in 1937 was parked against one of the two stone-based water towers sited at each end of the station.
REX CONWAY STEAM RAILWAY COLLECTION

ing the heavy, loaded wagons on the flat. The job of see-sawing back and forth should have been made easier by the engines' steam reversing gear, something of a novelty to Midland men. There was, however, a drawback in that it seems not to have been thought necessary to issue any maintenance instructions. As a result, nobody knew that there was a hydraulic control cylinder as well as the steam cylinder and, consequently, it was never filled with oil. George recalled that 'when the reverse control lever was moved over, the main reverse lever shot over with such a bang and a rattle that I marvelled that nobody got in the way of it and was maimed for life.'

During its sojourn at Wellingborough, 16920 was loaned to Kettering for a spell and, again, fortunately, some words of its activities have come to hand from a recent acquaintance with former Kettering loco-man, Bryan Benford. It was used on the Corby shunt, a Monday to Saturday turn, replacing standard 0–6–0T 7437. The engine obviously couldn't stay in Corby yard, some seven miles north of Kettering on the Manton line, all week without servicing so an exchange arrangement was diagrammed with the engine of the Manton pick-up. This was another daily turn which actually worked as far as Oakham, twenty-one miles distant, but detached and attached transfer traffic at Manton which was similarly handled by another pick-up from Peterborough. The Corby shunt engine left Kettering early on Monday morning and remained in the yard until late Tuesday afternoon. When the returning Manton pick-up pulled into the yard, its engine took up the shunting duties and the shunter brought the train back to Kettering and went onto the shed. Wednesday morning, refreshed, it went out again with the Manton and changed over with its rightful engine on arrival at Corby, allowing it to proceed to Oakham. This procedure was repeated on Thursday and Friday, each engine being away from the shed two days at a time. Crew relief for whichever engine was shunting was effected by enginemen travelling by train or bus to Corby & Weldon station and the engine running into the bay platform to make the changeover.

Bryan has also revealed that there was another 'foreigner' at Kettering in the same era, the former, 1929-built, Somerset & Dorset Sentinel 102 which became LMS 7191 in 1930. Few Sentinels were

No. 16913 was transferred to Wellingborough in February 1937 and is here seen inside one of the depot's two roundhouses. With his 'Austrian Goods' and 0–6–2Ts, Peter Drummond had introduced two, at the time, novel features: a fusible plug in the firebox and a hosepipe on the footplate. The latter on 16913, variously referred to as a slacking pipe or fizzle pipe, is clearly visible. COLLECTION R. J. ESSERY

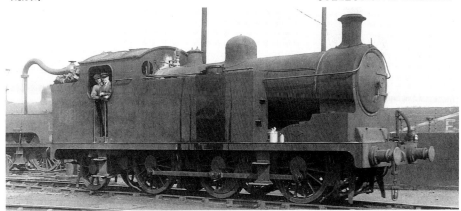

No. 16913 **again**, in a shed yard with the crew posed for the photograph. The driver was obviously disturbed in preparing the engine since his oil bottles were still on the foot framing. Behind the engine is the unmistakeable outline of a Midland 'Flatiron'. So far as I know, none was stationed at Wellingborough, although there were some on the District at Leicester. Perhaps one or other of the engines were taking a trip out? R. J. ESSERY

This undated but atmospheric photograph of 16920, the subject of the text, presents a poser: was the engine in Scotland or perhaps at Toton, Wellingborough or Kettering? Does the No. 2 target have any significance? Answers on a postcard please. Whatever, it was transferred to Hurlford in January 1942, and Kingmoor in November 1945, where it was withdrawn the following month. AUTHOR'S COLLECTION

included in the LMS locomotive list, unlike the LNER. Apart from the two S&D examples, there were only half a dozen others; two individual examples and four conventional two-speed models delivered in 1930 which, at the time, were numbered 7160–63 but became 7180–83 in 1939. One wonders why they were purchased at all but it seems that the company was concerned at the increasing cost of yard shunting and an appraisal exercise was being undertaken to reduce costs, parallel surveys being made with the early diesel shunters. 7191 on its home railway had been employed in and around colliery sidings at Radstock but its part in the studies was to be played out at Kettering in the extensive up sidings south of the station, displacing Midland 0–6–0T 1889.

There were two immediate advantages, the first being a lesser fuel consumption. The engine had only a small 12 cwt bunker but, on a good day's work used a bare 8 to 9 cwt, around half of that consumed by a conventional steam locomotive. Then there were the labour costs. Although double manned on the main line, as with other Sentinels it was single manned once in its area of operations and, what is more, the drivers received a lower rate of pay than their colleagues. If for no other reason, this was why 7191 was disliked by the drivers involved, of which Bryan's grandfather, Jack Rollins, was one. Several attempts were made to fail the engine and put it out of service. While travelling forward it would be put into

reverse and given steam to try and break the chain drive but to no avail.

Unconnected, perhaps, but more than once the firehole door of the vertical cross-tube boiler was fractured. Bill Thorley, who I knew as a Head Office Inspector at Euston in 1955, was a fitter at Wellingborough at the time and he was despatched on each occasion to fit a new door. His recollection is that the door was made from some alloy material which fractured rather easily and the door itself required to have a good seating on the firebox shell plate. (*A Breath of Steam*, Ian Allan, 1975.) He commented that 'these extramural activities were very welcome as they carried a shilling a day expenses if one could manage to spin out the job over the meal hour.'

When it came time for 7191 to leave and return to Radstock it was supposed to proceed light engine. To this end additional fuel supplies were organised by placing planks across the buffers and stacking them with coal. But again to no avail; the engine's water supply only lasted as far as Desborough and it was towed the rest of the way. Incidentally, I learn that the former Croyden Gas Works Sentinel, *Joyce*, works No. 7109 of 1927, virtually identical to the S&D pair, is hoped to be secured by the Somerset & Dorset Railway Heritage Trust for restoration and display as 101 at their Midsomer Norton South station.

S&DJR Sentinel 102 in its later BR guise as 47191 at Gloucester in June 1962. The vertical boiler seems to have occupied much of the cab space and it must have been a bit crowded when double manned. There was also a small coal bunker beside the boiler which, as with all Sentinels, was pressed to 275 psi – a pressure only surpassed on the LMS by 6399 Fury. On the S&DJR it had worked at Radstock, the low profile of the engine being required to clear the arch carrying the mineral railway up to Tyning Colliery. B. K. B. GREEN/INITIAL PHOTOGRAPHICS

No. 47191's former stablemate, S&DJR 101, in the shed yard at Radstock on 21st May 1929 in company with 0–6–0ST No. 7 which used to be employed on banking duties until ousted by the standard 3F 0–6–0Ts. It is my understanding that the Somerset & Dorset Heritage Trust hope to acquire the former Croydon Gas Works Sentinel, a near double, for restoration and display as 101 at Midsomer Norton.
H. C. CASSERLEY

LMS SIGNALS

No. 17 – An Introduction to Colour Light and Power Signalling

by L. G. WARBURTON

THIS article is not intended to be a definitive history on this subject, but to serve as an introduction and an indication as to where the LMS stood in this field, before going on to consider the re-signalling schemes carried out by the Company involving colour light signals and power frames.

COLOUR LIGHT SIGNALS

In their book *Modern Railway Signalling*, M. G. Tweedie and T. S. Lascelles stated 'The earliest light signal is by tradition reported to have been a candle burning in the window of a point watcher's house, it having been agreed with drivers that the presence of a light meant they were to stop'.

With the widespread availability of electricity, it is generally considered that colour light signalling originated in America and that one of the first installations on a main line was on the Pennsylvania, Tunnel and Terminal Corporation in 1910. However, in Britain, a system of colour and position lights was devised by Thomas Forsyth around 1845. From that date it was not until 1913 that the matter was seriously taken up again by A. E. Tattersall who experimented with light systems.

The case for colour light signalling is very strong and based on sound arguments.

The semaphore signal
- Shows different indications by day and night.
- Its location and background must be carefully considered if a good indication is to be seen.
- There is a multiplicity of moving parts to be affected by adverse weather.
- Little or no indication can be seen in such conditions as fog and falling snow.

Against this, colour light signals
- Have few or no moving parts.
- They give a better light against poor backgrounds.
- They can be sited at driver's eye level.
- They give a strong indication in fog and snow.
- They are easily adapted to 2, 3, 4 and 5 aspect systems.

There were various types of colour light signals with varying voltages and power, but by 1935 there were three types of colour light signals generally in use by the LMS:
- (1) Multi-unit 24 watts.
- (2) Searchlight 12 watts.
- (3) Searchlight 3.3 watts.

Of these (1) gave the best dispersion and was therefore most suitable for use when the approach was on a curve, but each could be fitted with a 'Spreadlite' lens to meet special cases, but the use of such lenses considerably reduces the range. In order that fog signalmen could be dispensed with, either (1) or (2) had to be used. When (2) or (3) were used, the operation of the coloured vane within the signal head had to be repeated to the signalman or alternatively proved. This was due to the 'Searchlight' signal consisting of a single lamp with moving spectacles for changing the aspect, with the consequent disadvantage of having moving parts, although it had in its favour the ability to be trained and focused on a particular line to ease the driver's recognition (*Plate 4*). The multi-aspect signal has separate lamps and no moving parts and it cannot be trained on a particular line of vision as the distance between the top and bottom light is too great.

One further big advantage colour lights have over the semaphore system is the ease with which automatic signalling can be installed using track circuiting, brought about by the aspects being determined by whether wheels are short circuiting across the rails.

It is probably fair to say that until Signal and Telegraph Departments were consolidated, progress on power schemes would not have been easy as mechanical signalling came under the Civil Engineer and electrical matters were the responsibility of either the Electrical Engineer or the CME. This obviously meant two separate departments were involved with likely conflict of opinion; consider the scenario if an isolated semaphore distant signal was to be replaced by a colour light signal.

Apart from tube railways, the first daylight colour light system in this country was on the Liverpool Overhead Railway, which came into use in April 1921, being a 2-aspect system. The only other examples of multi-aspect signalling were three-position semaphores on the GWR Ealing, and Shepherds Bush section, GCR Keadby Bridge (eight signals), GNR Kings Cross (three signals) and SE&CR Victoria Station, London. In none of these schemes was there any special feature beyond the 3-aspect principle, whereby each signal was a repeater of the one next ahead, and, as only one installation was on each railway, there was no risk of confusion with ordinary signalling.

The first 3-aspect colour light installation was brought into use on the GCR in April 1923 between Marylebone and Neasden although Marylebone and Neasden Junctions remained mechanically worked.

Progress after that date was rapid, particularly on the Southern Railway which was the only system to have an overall plan and policy covering colour light installation, this being due to the complex lines inherited south of the Thames after the 1923 grouping. On other railways, colour lights only appeared at points where semaphores were definitely inferior, or required renewal, revisions to track layout were made or there was a need to increase the frequency of trains, i e. run more trains per hour.

The first 4-aspect system was introduced on the Southern Railway between Holborn Viaduct and Elephant and Castle in 1926, followed by other installations in the London Area. (See table for a listing of major company installations from 1923 to 1947.)

The first LMS 4-aspect installation was the Manchester Victoria and Exchange scheme of 1929.

Consider now the various colour light aspects:

2-Aspect

This arrangement simply substituted the indications given by semaphore signals. It did at least give the same indications by day and by night, eliminated signal wire runs, made fog signalmen unnecessary and increased line capacity. The Bow Road to

Barking scheme brought into use in February 1928 is an LMS example.

A colour light can be operated mechanically by simply placing an electric light bulb behind the spectacle plate of a semaphore signal – as was done by the LMS. This may also involve removing the arm, or fitting a shortened arm and replacing the spectacle glass with a form of lens; the LMS used a Corning Lebby Lens, the assembly being known as 'Intensified lighting'.

Proceeding now to multiple aspect systems, defining 'Multi-Aspect Signalling' as any system involving more than 2 aspects.

3-Aspect

Red, yellow or green is the same as the normal semaphore indications, i.e. Red – Stop; Yellow – be prepared to stop at the next signal, and Green – Proceed (*Plate 5*).

4-Aspect

With this system the double yellow is introduced, giving the indication 'Attention, run at medium speed'. This is followed by a signal giving a single yellow indication, indicating the next signal is at danger, (red).

It can be seen that with three- or four-aspect signalling, every signal can be a distant or caution signal, thus track occupation can be considerably increased.

Now when considering the semaphore distant displaying green for 'off', this means that not only is the next signal 'off', but so too are several other successive signals so that generally the line clear is to the next signal box in advance, which may well be five miles away. Put another way, there can only be one train between adjacent signal boxes with the block system, but with three- or four-aspect signalling, track occupation can be considerably increased.

The Southern Railway identified the four-aspect system as particularly beneficial as its electric trains running at slower speeds and fitted with Westinghouse braking could run up to full speed up to the single yellow indication. On the other hand, the faster-running vacuum-braked steam express running on the same line would need to commence braking on sight of the double yellow aspect.

With close train headways, it is quite possible to run long distances and never see a green signal aspect.

5-Aspect

This introduced the aspect of Yellow over Green indicating – Pass second signal at restricted speed. This was only used on the LMS Mirfield re-signalling scheme to be described in a later part of this series. However, Bound did point out that it may require further consideration should high-speed running become normal, as with the 'Coronation Scot', due to the siting of many distant signals giving insufficient stopping distance to the stop signal ahead.

Position Lights

Position lights were adopted by the Pennsylvania Railroad in 1910 having horizontal, inclined and vertical rows of white lights for danger, caution and clear respectively, with the first one being tried on the Metropolitan Railway in 1918.

The first position-light ground signals were installed in the Cape Town re-signalling scheme in South Africa in 1928 (*Plate 14*), and were first used in the UK in connection with the re-signalling of the LNER York–Northallerton main line in 1932 (*Plate 13*). They consisted of two horizontal white lights indicating danger ('on') with two white lights inclined at 45 degrees indicating clear ('off'). The idea behind using white lights was that a driver could pass the two horizontal white lights when a main aspect was 'off', the principle being that drivers should not pass red lights. Later, when one red light was substituted as part of the 'on' indication, it became necessary for the main route to clear to clear any position lights in the route.

The inspecting officer Lt. Col. A. H. L. Mount was not impressed and neither were the opinions of other officers unanimous. Accordingly, it was agreed that the forty or so position lights on this scheme be placed on a conditional trial for two years, at the end of which a standard would hopefully be agreed. Other ground signals in contention were the colour light shunt signal used by the Southern Railway, shunting disc signals (red bar on a white disc), banner signals, etc. In the event, the position light won the day with disc type retained on mechanical installations.

Position-light high-speed route indication was again pioneered by the North Eastern Area of the LNER which used a chain of five white lights that were illumi-nated to indicate to the driver that a diverging route was set. The Southern Railway soon followed suit using three lights. The five-light arrangement is now the British standard, often referred to as 'feathers'.

TRACK CIRCUITS

Before moving on to types of power frames, it is important to consider track circuiting, as although early power schemes such as Glasgow Central, in 1907, boasted the largest installation with 374 levers, it was devoid of any track circuiting.

Track circuits have contributed more than anything else to the means of running a railway. The principle is very simple, consisting of an electric current flowing in each rail with a relay connected across the rails energised by the current flowing. The presence of a train causes a short circuit, resulting in the relay being de-energized, thus closing contacts on the relay that can then, using lamps on the signal box diagram, indicate the presence of a train. In addition the track circuit relay will actuate an electric lock on the signal lever, making it impossible to work the signal that would allow a train into the section should one already be there. It is also fail-safe, as should the electricity supply fail, the relay will give a track occupied indication.

Until the advent of full track circuiting, it was necessary for a signalman to see all trains, which meant that a power box generally replaced a mechanical signal box. However, once track circuits were proved to be totally reliable, it became possible to construct a signal box diagram with sections of track illuminated by lamps lit by a train occupying that particular section. It then became possible for one power box to replace several mechanical signal boxes as the signalman could check the progress of a train without actually seeing it.

An American – William Robinson – produced the first track circuit in 1871, and in Britain, following an accident in 1884 on the Great Eastern Railway at Stepney, the Inspecting Officer, Major General Hutchinson suggested the Company should install a track circuit, which was not done. The first British track circuit was installed at St. Paul's by W. R. Sykes in 1886.

Little progress was made in Britain until the Hawes Junction disaster on 24th June

1910 gave impetus for track circuit installation. Two light engines were stood at the signal, and, with a failure to carry out rule 55, the presence of the engines slipped the signalman's mind, who then accepted a Scotch express. The light engines moved off, thinking the signal was for them, only to be hit in the rear by the express. The Midland Railway then identified some 2,000 other places where similar accidents could occur and commenced track circuit installation, becoming the company with the most track circuits installed.

Track circuiting was later used for the simple control of purely automatic signals, and then refined for use at busy and complex junctions, providing many additional safeguards to those found on a mechanically-locked lever frame.

Baker Street station on the Metropolitan Railway showed what could be done with its power interlocking installed in 1913. Track circuits controlled the signals that were provided with train stops. The signal box not only controlled the lines visible to the signalman but also those that were not, being the junction with the Inner Circle line which was in a tunnel at the far end of the station, achieved by indications on an illuminated diagram.

POWER FRAMES

Power signalling may be defined as 'any method of operating points and signals avoiding a mechanical system of rods or wires'.

Not every installation of colour light signalling was necessarily a power scheme, e.g. when the main running lines at Rugby were re-signalled in 1939 with colour lights by the LMS, the existing six mechanical signal boxes were retained together with mechanical operation of all points; on the other hand, Crewe was re-signalled about the same time in 1940, as a power scheme, with two new power boxes and Westinghouse-style 'L' all-electric frames. The Mirfield 'Speed' installation of 1932 retained the signal boxes and the mechanical operation of points but with five-aspect colour light signalling. All these schemes will be discussed in this series.

Power operation has many advantages over operation by conventional lever frames, including:

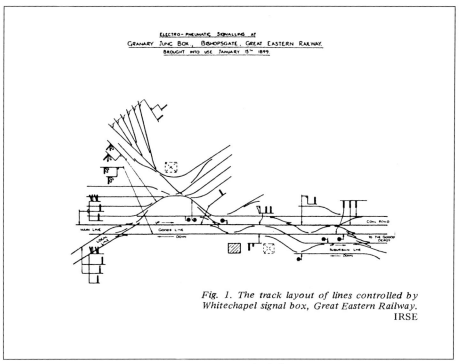

Fig. 1. The track layout of lines controlled by Whitechapel signal box, Great Eastern Railway.
IRSE

* No restriction in the distance a signal or point can be from the signal box. Mechanical limits were, in the first instance, 180 yards for facing points (300 yards for trailing), gradually increased to 350 yards for points. Double-wire working increased the distance points could be operated from the signal box to around 700 yards, LMS installations in passenger lines being at Blackwell, Stoke Works, Mansfield Colliery and Rufford Colliery. The maximum wire pull for signals was about 2,000 yards, usually the distant signal.
* Unaffected by variations in temperature. Wire tensioners were often to be found in signal boxes to adjust signal wires affected by heat and cold (expansion and contraction).
* Rodding and wire runs often needed protection to avoid trips and falls by staff as required by The Railway Employment (Prevention of Accidents) Act of 1901.
* Point rollers and wire pulleys required maintenance and adjustment.
* At complex installations or anywhere space was limited, great difficulty could be experienced in arranging 'lead offs' for signals and points adjacent to the signal box.
* With operating distance no longer a consideration, it is possible to abolish signal boxes with the consequent saving in staff wages, e.g. a triangular junction could be worked from one box instead of the usual three.

No physical effort is required to work the box, when previously a considerable effort could be needed for the distant signal or a point fitted with an economical facing point lock and locking bar. A disadvantage may be due to complexity, more highly-trained maintenance staff are required.

Many 'power' systems have been used over the years, the main ones being electro-pneumatic, electro-mechanical and differing types of all-electric. A hydraulic system was devised by Bianchi & Servettaz and used in Russia, France, India and South Africa (*Plate 16*), but not, as far as I am aware, in Great Britain.

These power systems utilized a miniature lever frame in conjunction with a conventional signal box diagram to activate points and signals, that is, until the advent of the 'control panel' type of arrangement, whereby switches controlling points and signals were mounted on the diagram itself, thereby eliminating any kind of lever, the interlocking being achieved by electrical means.

The power operation of points and signals could also be affected by a conventional lever frame suitably modified to activate electrical switches, relays, etc. A simple example of this is when an outlying distant signal was either motor-worked or replaced by a colour light. In such cases the lever operating any power-worked signal or point would be shortened to save the signalman falling backwards having expected a heavy 'pull'.

Electro-Pneumatic

Patented by Westinghouse and first used in America in 1884, it was McKenzie and Holland who installed the first British installation on goods lines at Granary Junction near Bishopsgate on the Great Eastern Railway and brought into use on 15th January 1899, displacing two older boxes (*Plate 1 and Fig. 1*). The frame was

Plate 1. *Whitechapel signal box on the Great Eastern Railway, containing a 38-lever electro-pneumatic frame, being the first such installation in Great Britain, albeit on goods lines. The mechanical tappet locking is immediately behind the levers with the electrical controlling contacts in the middle and the electric locks in the rear. The frame was manufactured by the Union Switch and Signal Co. USA and installed by McKenzie and Holland Ltd. in 1898.*

Plate 2. *Electro-pneumatic signals at Bolton, which, in 1903, was the first installation on a passenger line and also the first instance of a triangular junction being controlled from one box – Bolton West. The box was equipped with an 80-working-lever frame supplied by the Westinghouse Brake and Saxby Signal Co. The signals and points were operated by compressed air at a pressure of 70/80 psi, controlled electrically from the frame, hence the term 'electro-pneumatic'. The scheme was designed by C. B. Byles, the L&Y Signal Superintendent and obviously considered to be a success as Southport was re-signalled in 1919 and Blackpool in 1921 using the same method.*

the second of two European imports manufactured by the Union Switch and Signal Co. of the USA (Westinghouse), following which frames were made by McKenzie and Holland.

Points, facing point locks and detectors, signals, and crossing gates are operated by compressed air by means of small cylinders or 'motors' fixed on the apparatus to be worked. The valves admitting the compressed air to the motors are opened and shut by means of electro-magnets. Locking was achieved by switches interlocked by means of tappet locks, similar to an ordinary locking frame, the levers having 2½in centres. An air supply is required to points and signals for which a power house is necessary, equipped with air compressors and motors to drive them.

The Lancashire and Yorkshire Railway installed an electro-pneumatic system at Bolton in 1903 (*Plate 2*), Southport in 1919 and Blackpool in 1921. Glasgow Central was re-signalled by the Caledonian Railway, using this system in 1908. The North Eastern, Great Western and Great Central Railways also had installations. In all cases the signals were semaphores.

The LMS did not utilize this system in any of its schemes, although electro-pneumatic was the method chosen when British Rail re-signalled Euston in 1952, using Westinghouse equipment, including a style 'L' all-electric frame.

Electric Systems

There were two basic methods of electrical operation of points and signals, one using solenoids, the other using electric motors. The advent of colour light signals obviously eliminated the need for any kind of motor for signal operation. Note the term 'all-electric' is misleading in that the interlocking arrangements were still effected mechanically until the arrival of electric relay interlocking.

Crewe 'All-Electric' System

This was designed and patented (12128 17th May 1897) by Francis William Webb and Arthur Moore Thompson of the LNWR and whilst extensive layouts were provided at Crewe, Euston and Manchester London Road (now Piccadilly), only one installation was ever made elsewhere and that on the North Eastern Railway at Severus Junction, York. The system was manufactured by the Railway Signal Company of Fazakerly, Liverpool. It was a DC system of 100 or

Plate 3. *The 'Crewe All-Electric' system. An LNWR single-post semaphore signal at Camden operated by a 220 volt DC solenoid motor mounted beneath the arm.*
NATIONAL RAILWAY MUSEUM (D196)

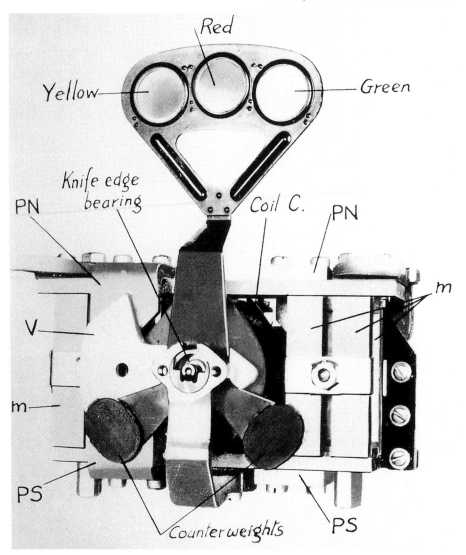

Plate 4. *A searchlight signal movement showing the yellow, red and green moving vanes balanced on a knife-edged bearing with counterweights ensuring the signal showed red in case of failure. The first searchlight signals to be installed in this country were by A. F. Bound when the new LNER loop from Neasden was constructed to serve Wembley Stadium. At this time the searchlight colour light signal was manufactured solely by the Hall Switch & Signal Co. of America. Later, they were manufactured, under licence, by the Siemens and General Electric Signal Co. of East Lane, Wembley. Multi-head signals had no moving parts and eventually superseded this design.*

Plate 5. *A 3-aspect day colour light head showing the sidelights ('pigs ears') having a range of at least 5,000 feet.*

220 volts. The locking frame consisted of two tiers of miniature levers at 1¾in centres. The mechanical tappet locking was carried out below floor level by light rods attached to the lever tails. Signals were operated by electro-magnets with points by electro-magnets or electric motors. The first installation was at Gresty Lane, Crewe, consisting of 57 levers brought into use in December 1898. LMS Signal Engineers Bound and Morgan hated the system, but nevertheless did not immediately replace it, and it was the pioneer all-electric system (*Plate 3*).

[With the editor's permission, this system will be considered later as it is beyond the scope of this series.]

All-Electric

This was manufactured by several firms such as Siemens, Westinghouse, British Power Railway Signal Company, General Railway Signal Company, etc, all using miniature lever frames with interlocking carried out via mechanical tappet locking or, later on, electrically. The system could operate conventional semaphores using electric motors (as at Newport GWR in 1927) or, more usually, colour light signals with point operation by electric motors.

Westinghouse supplied their last mechanically-locked 'K' frame in 1935 with the last but one order by a British main-line railway being used on the LMS Manchester Victoria and Exchange resignalling brought into full use on 24th March 1929 (*Plate 6*). Mechanically-locked all-electric power frames remained the policy on the London Underground.

The first truly all-electric frame in Britain (*Plate 7*) (e.g. dispensing with mechanical locking) was installed at North Kent East junction (*Plate 8*) on the Southern Railway and brought into use on 1st December 1929. Clearly a signalman is not concerned with how his frame is locked; whether by mechanical means or through a de-energized electro-magnet, the lever cannot be pulled.

The advantage of the all-electric frame was that levers were not required to be in one continuous row. Frames could be constructed in sections, resulting in signal boxes of reduced size.

The first use of such a frame on the LMS was at Glasgow St. Enoch, commissioned on 14th May 1933.

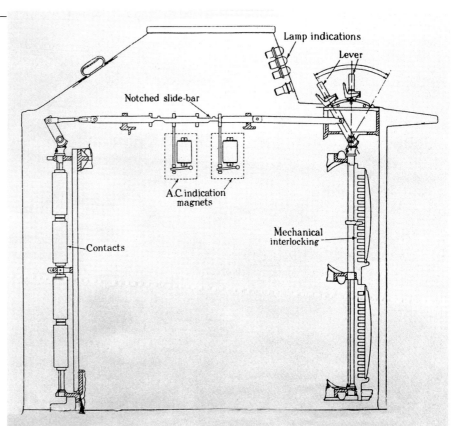

Plate 6. *A cross-section of the Westinghouse Style 'K' mechanically-locked power frame which was in use until c.1929.*

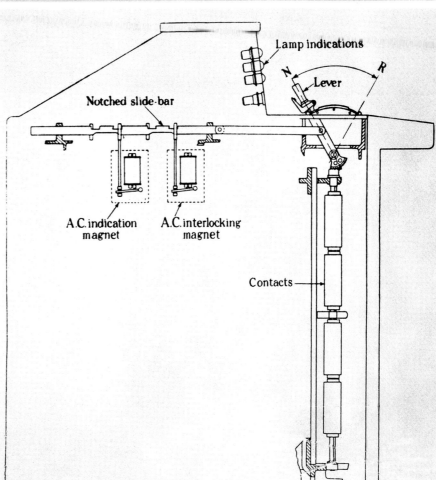

Plate 7. *A cross-section of the Westinghouse Style 'L' electrically-locked power frame which superseded the Style 'K' frame.*

Plate 8. *North Kent East Junction Westinghouse Style 'L' power frame, being the first 'all-electric' power frame to be installed in Great Britain, having 83 levers and commissioned in 1929.*

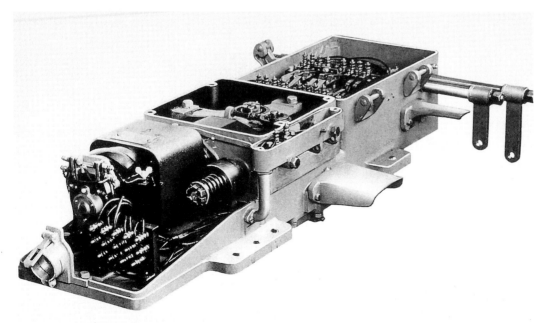

Plate 9. *A Westinghouse Style 'M3' electric point machine with the case removed. The 'M'3 was developed from the 'M', of which over 1,200 were manufactured from c.1923 onwards. The standard voltages were 20/25v, 100/110v DC or 100/110v AC, the operating speed being about 3.5 seconds.*

Plate 10. *Thirsk control panel was considered to be the first installation where miniature levers were dispensed with by a combined switch and diagram embodying the route system. The area covered was 4½ geographical miles, which was the largest in the UK at the time, with five mechanical boxes being dispensed with. The British Power Railway Signal Co. were the main contractors, others being Siemens and the General Electric Railway Signal Co. The panel was brought into use on 19th November 1933.*

Control Panel

With the change from mechanical locking to electric locking, the next step was the elimination of the actual lock on the lever, resulting in its replacement by a simple thumb switch, and whilst the switch could be turned, the electric relays prevented any response to the operation. Miniature levers were dispensed with, signals and points being operated utilizing a combined switch and diagram.

Route Relay Interlocking

Route relay interlocking was pioneered by A. E. Tattersall on the North Eastern Area of the LNER; the first scheme was small and controlled the approaches to the Goole swing bridge.

The second, and much larger scheme was at Thirsk and covered 4½ geographical miles, the longest in Britain at the time. Even by 1939 no other country in the world had any route interlocking of the magnitude of Thirsk. A conventional power frame would have required 170 levers, about 24ft 0in long, the Thirsk panel being some 12ft 0in in length (*Plate 10 & Fig. 2*). With point switching, it was now possible, using just one thumb

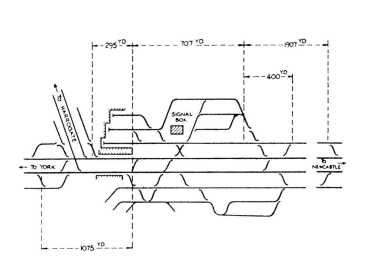

TRACK LAYOUT AT THIRSK, L.N.E.R.

Fig. 2. The track layout at Thirsk before being increased to four tracks at the York end.

IRSE

Plate 11. *The North-allerton control panel, which was similar to Thirsk, was the first to incorporate white route lights and brought into use on 3rd September 1939.*

switch, to operate all relevant points on the route set, and when electrically proved, the appropriate signals also. In one case at Thirsk, 14 pairs of points and one signal were operated in 6 seconds by one switch, the switches being mounted on the actual signal box diagram.

Route relay interlocking was gradually enlarged in that Northallerton contained 129 routes, Hull Paragon 230 routes, and the 1939 York scheme had no less than 825 routes, although with war intervention it was not completed until 1951.

With later installations such as Hull Paragon in 1938, it became desirable to separate the switches from the diagram, the switches being on a console with the illuminated diagram behind.

With large installations covering numerous routes, it was necessary to convey to other signalmen the route(s) set, which was achieved by a chain of white lights being illuminated for the route set, first used at Northallerton in 1938 (*Plate 11*).

The LMS used the idea in part at Wigan in 1941 where signals were operated using similar thumb switches but points retained conventional lever frames and the route relay system was not employed.

As a matter of historical interest, the Thirsk scheme was on the East Coast

Plate 12. *The re-signalling of the Southern line between Waterloo and Hampton Court Junction in 1936 used three-lamp position light high-speed junction route indicators (the LNER using five lamps) more usually known as 'feathers'. Also a first on this scheme was the use of sidelights on the colour light head, allowing the driver to draw up alongside the signal and still see the indication displayed, referred to by railwaymen as 'pigs ears'.*

Plate 13. *A position light ground signal at Leeds East in 1936. Two white lights are exhibited horizontally for danger ('on'), with two diagonal white lights for proceed ('off'). They were equipped with backlights and those signals leading to trap points included one red light. Standard 110v AC high-voltage lamps were used behind a lens combination including a pale blue glass, giving an excellent indication by day, reduced to half voltage at night. The position light featured here leads to a Westinghouse electro-pneumatic derailer and therefore includes a red light.*

Plate 14. *Position light ground signals were first installed at Cape Town in 1928, as seen here with CT43 and 44. The picture is taken looking towards Cape Town station with the wall of the Castle of Good Hope on the left. The castle is the oldest colonial building in South Africa built between 1666 and 1679 by the Dutch East India Company, better known as the VOC (Vereenigde Oost-Indische Compagnie). Since the picture was taken, the 'Strand' highway runs between the fort and the railway. The new signal box, built for the re-signalling, can just be seen at the far end of the wall that contained a Westinghouse Style 'K' 143-lever power frame No. L30, replacing the Bianchi & Servettas hydraulic power frame in the old box.*

Plate 15. *The hand generator installed in Chesterton Junction signal box on the LNER which controlled three signals and three points; all were around 1,000 yards or more from the box, the equipment being supplied by Westinghouse and commissioned in 1932.*

Main Line between Alne and Green Lane Signal Box (Thirsk) which was previously equipped with track circuit and automatic signals installed by the Hall Signal Co. in 1903. It was the second such scheme, the first being Andover–Grateley on 20th April 1902. As the latter was dispensed with in WWI, the Alne/Thirsk was the oldest. It had two original features: (1) Signals were operated by carbon dioxide gas (CO2) at high pressure in cylinders at the foot of the post, which was released to put the signal 'off', control led by relays. (2) The signals normally stood at danger, and, providing the section ahead and its overlap were unoccupied, an approaching train put its own signals to 'clear'.

The GWR first used route switching at Winchester in 1922 and later with a larger installation at Newport in 1927. In these installations the principal was incorporated in a power frame with interlocking between levers being mechanical. The signals were semaphores operated by electric motors as were the points.

Entrance-Exit System

A different form of route relay interlocking was devised by the Metropolitan Vickers General Railway Signal Co. with the world's first installation being at Brunswick on the Cheshire Lines Committee (*Plate 17*). Two movements

Plate 16. *Salt River signal box at Cape Town, showing the Bianchi & Servettas hydraulic power frame, not a type used in Great Britain but included for interest. The frame was replaced in 1932 by a Westinghouse Style 'L' all-electric frame (L54) having 71 levers in a new signal box.*

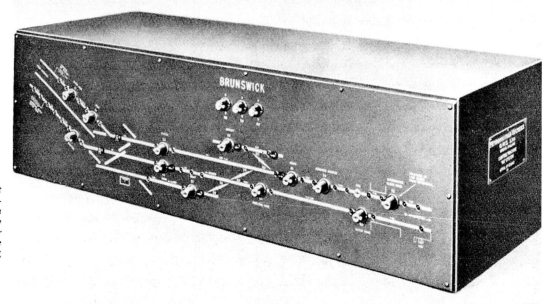

Plate 17. *The world's first entrance/exit panel manufactured by Metropolitan Vickers General Railway Signal Co. in 1939 for Brunswick on the Cheshire Lines Railway.* IRSE

Item	Company	Date	Scheme	Power Frame	C/L Head	Aspects	Remarks
1	Liverpool O/H Rly.	1921	Re-signalling	Automatic		2	The first in the UK.
2	LNER/GCR	1923	Marylebone - Neasdon		Hall Single Hd.	3	The "Hall" head was forerunner to the "searchlight"
3	LNER	1926	Cambridge	BPRS	Semaphore	2	All-Electric (Mech. Locked); Cam.N. 72L; Cam.S. 128L;5 Abolished.
4	LNER	1931	York - Northallerton	BPRS	Searchlight	4	Thirsk SB - 1st.Panel with Thumb Switches: Northallerton 1st. Illuminated. Diag.
5	LNER	1932	Highgate Branch			?	
6	LNER	1933	Bethnall Green - Enfield			?	
7	LNER	1933	Gidea Park - Shenfield		Searchlight, 2 Heads	4	
8	LNER	1933	Kings Cross	Siemens	In-line	4	All Elec. Min.lever frame 232L; Motor Op. Ground Sigs. (1st.Track-circuit in UK in tunnel-1894).
9	LNER	1934	Hull Paragon		Searchlight, 2 Heads	?	Electro-Pneumatic Points & Signals.
10	LNER	1935	Fenchurch Street - Bow Rd.	Siemens	In-line	4	140L. Elec. Locking.
11	LNER/LMS Joint	1936	Leeds New (LNER Designed).		Searchlight	4	Leeds East; E/P; Points Mech. Worked; Relay Locking:
12	LNER/LMS Joint	1936	ditto		Searchlight	4	Leeds West; Sig. & Point Op. by Thumb Switches.
13	GWR	1927	Newport	Siemens	Semaphore	2	79L. Working motor operated semaphore signals & points. Ferreira/Insell Route system
14	GWR	1929	Old Oak Common			?	
15	GWR	1931	Paddington - Southall	Gen.Rly.Sig.Co	Searchlight, 2 Heads	2	All-Elec.Lock'g.- Westbourne Br.88L(1st.on GWR).;Mech. Lock'g. Padd'n. Arr.184L.; Dep.96L.
16	GWR	1933	Cardiff East	West. "L"	Searchlight, 2 Heads	2	Elec.Lock'g-153L.
17	GWR	1934	Cardiff West	West. "L"	Searcligh, 2 Headst	2	Elec.Lock'g-339L
18	GWR	1935	Bristol Temple Meads	Gen.Rly.Sig.Co	Searchlight	2	T.M.East 368L.; T.M.West 328L.; Btol.Loco.Yd.32L.; Largest in UK in No.of levers
19	GWR	1940	Reading	Siemens		?	
20	Southern Rly	1926	Holborne Via. - Elephant & Castle	Siemens 86L	In-line	4	1st. 4 Aspect scheme in the world.
21	Southern Rly	1926	Charing Cross - Cannon Street	West. "K"	In-line & cluster	4	Char.X.107L.; Met.J. 60M. Convtd.; Can.St.143L.
22	Southern Rly	1926	Ditto-extended to London Br.		In-line & Cluster	4	
23	Southern Rly	1929	Lon.Br. - G'wich/L'ham/Parks Br.J.	West. "L"	In-line & cluster	4	N.Kent.E.J. 1st."L" Elec.Lock.83L F.; Lon.Br.311L"K"Fr.; Other boxes mech F.s.
24	Southern Rly	1932	Coulsdon - Brighton	West. "L"	In-line	4	Brighton 225L Elec. Locking; All other boxes Mech. Frames.
25	Southern Rly	1936	Waterloo - Hampton Court Junc.	West. "L"	In-line	4	W'loo 309L; Clap.Junc.103L.; W.Lon.59L.; 1st use of 'Feathers' 'Side lights'.
26	Southern Rly	1938	Victoria - Clapham Junc.	West. "L"	In-line	4	Vic.225L; Vic.A. 200L. Adapted; Battersea Pk.31L.
27	LMS	1928	Bow Road - Barking	None	In-line	2	1st.application of West.Style"D"Lever Locks in mech SBs.
28	LMS	1929	Manchester Victoria & Exchange	West. "K"	In-line& cluster	4	Vic.W.85L.; Deal St.91L.; Irwell Br. Sdgs.12L.
29	LMS	1932	Barking - Upminster	None	Searchlight	2	Marker lights. Mech.SBs(mod).
30	LMS	1932	Mirfield	None	Searchlight	5	Marker lights. Mech.SBs(mod).
31	LMS	1933	Euston - Watford	None	Searchlight	4	Marker lights. Mech.SBs(mod).
32	LMS	1933	Glasgow - St. Enoch	West. "L"	Searchlight	4	Marker lights. 1st."L" frame on LMS 203 L.
33	LMS	1939	Rugby	None	In-line	4	5 light Rl.s; 7 Mech.SBs (6 mod).
34	LMS	1940	Crewe	West."L"	In-line	4	5 light Rl.s; Crewe N.,S, A, B.
35	LMS	1941	Wigan	None	In-line	4	5 light Rl.s; 3 New SBs with thumb switches & REC Frames; (7Abolished).
36	LMS	1942	Willesden No.7 - North Wembley	?	In line	4	
37	LMS	1943	Camden No.2 - Willesden No.1	?	In line	4	
38	LMS	1945	Camden No.2 - Euston No.2	?	In-line	4	
39	LMS	1946	Liverpool Exchange	?	In-line	?	
40	LMS	1948	Liverpool Lime Street	?	In line	4	5 light Rl.s;
41	Metropolitan Rly.	1932	Wembley Park & Stanmore Branch	West. "L"	In-line	3	2nd."L" frame in UK 93L 1st. Installation of Centralized Traffic Control (CTC) in UK (4 1/2 Miles).

are required by the signalman to set up a route. Switches are placed at each signal on the illuminated diagram, and, to set up a route the signalman presses a button at the 'entrance' and the button at the 'exit'. If the conditions are in order, with no conflicting routes already set and the track circuits unoccupied, the points are set for that route and the signal at the entrance cleared. Again the war intervened and the much larger installations at Stratford and Bow could not be completed until the war was over.

Hand Generation

Situations could arise where a manned signal box was required, say a mile away from another signal box, simply to work a branch line, required only because the maximum run for point rodding was 350 yards. To obviate this and enable the junction signal box to be dispensed with, a hand generator was devised and patented jointly by Messrs Nicholson and Roberts of the Great Southern Railway of Ireland, making 100 volts available for the operation of points and semaphore signals.

The first installation was at Charleville on the GSR of I, where, as a result of political activity, the junction signal box to Limerick was not rebuilt but signalled from Charleville, a distance of 1850 yards. The LNER installed several sets (*Plate 15*), the LMS generally preferring to use the double wire system.

SUMMARY

So where did the LMS fit into the development of colour light and power signalling? Arguably, the Company was first in loco and carriage design, but with regard to colour light and power signalling, probably third, although it is fair to state that such schemes had to be financially justified with reasonable returns set against capital expenditure.

As stated, the Southern Railway was the only one with any form of policy. it installed the first 4-aspect system, the first all-electric frame, and was the first to use side lights on signals, enabling a driver to draw right up to the signal and still view its indication via side lights on the signal head (although a similar arrangement was incorporated on the Manchester Victoria and Exchange scheme).

The London and North Eastern Railway took a major leap forward with the installation at Thirsk, which was the first to dispense with levers, with operation being via switches on a diagram, the forerunner of today's 'panel'. The LNER also introduced white route lights on the Northallerton panel introduced on 3rd September 1939 and the position light ground signal as well as the five-light high-speed route indicator.

Both the above companies pioneered several things that were to become the standard, for colour light and power signalling, e.g. a 4-aspect system on the Southern and the use of diagrams or panels in lieu of any kind of lever frames on the LNER.

The LMS was certainly not oblivious to the new technology, bearing in mind it was Dound, who, as an employee of the Great Central Railway, put into place the Marylebone–Neasden 3-aspect scheme; also he was resident engineer when the London and South Western Railway installed automatic signalling on the line between Andover and Grateley. It must be remembered that there was no 'code of practice' to follow and therefore railway companies were well aware of the cost savings, etc, to be made with the adoption of power signalling; it was simply a fact that various ideas had to be tried and tested, with the best eventually becoming the standard.

The LMS was quick to use 4 aspects at Manchester and an all-electric frame at St. Enoch, it also pioneered the 5-aspect Mirfield scheme and marker lights, but these latter two ideas proved not to be the way ahead. Once the 4-aspect standard was set, the LMS pursued it vigorously with the re-signalling of Rugby, Wigan, Crewe North and South, etc, all of which will be dealt with later in this series. The LMS did pioneer such things as 'last wheel replacement' and 'sectional release route locking', to be described in the appropriate part within this series.

With the exception of Plates 3 & 17, all photographs are courtesy of Westinghouse.

A label for traffic from Ireland via the Belfast and Northern Counties Railway to Cambridge. Readers will find this potential traffic is referred to in Stanley Jenkins' article on the Portpatrick and Wigtownshire Joint Line at page 67. (Editor)

LMS
TERRITORY

In this issue we begin to tell the story of the Lickey Incline and it seemed to me that it would make sense to show readers what the approach to the Lickey looked like from the north. This picture was taken from the footbridge at Barnt Green in 1949 and is looking towards Blackwell station some 1 mile 35 chains to the south-west. The summit of the old Birmingham and Gloucester line is between Barnt Green and Blackwell and the gradient section will be found at page 5. For westbound trains the line was 'against the engine' from Burton to the summit, then it was 'with the engine' to Eckington, followed by a slight rise to Bredon and a fall to Ashchurch, then uphill to Cheltenham. This picture shows the main-line platforms; the branch line platforms were to the left of the picture. The layout of the station at Barnt Green changed over the years but readers who may be interested in the changes will find they are recorded in Ashchurch to Barnt Green, the Evesham Route *by R. J. Essery, published by OPC.*

J. H. MOSS

Through the Carriage Window

by KEITH MILES

DURING forty years of railway service and for many years before and since, I have spent countless hours travelling by train and enjoyed the passing scene through the carriage windows. Throughout these journeys certain features stood out both physically and of personal interest. Two in particular, from opposite ends of the country were of lasting attraction, but first, as former wireless football commentators used to say, back to square one.

I started regular train travel early in September 1938 as a new pupil at Hemel Hempstead Grammar School. My attention, as I progressed from King's Langley, was immediately drawn to the new station under construction at Apsley for the use of the thousands of employees who worked at the adjacent John Dickinson paper mills. Dickinson purchased the original mill in 1809, acquired Nash Mills two years later and built Home Park Mill at King's Langley in 1820. When King's Langley station was first opened in 1841, at the suggestion of John Dickinson, it was a simple wooden structure known briefly as Home Park Halt; the subsequent brick-built structures didn't appear until 1896. Nash Mills gave its name to a signal box but this became an intermediate block post in my time. The new Apsley station was also instigated by Dickinson's and was opened, rather dramatically, on 22nd September 1938 by Watford's 2446, at the head of a down local, driving through a sheet of the company's 'Lion Brand' paper stretched across the track. The station was constructed in the art deco style which was reflected in the architecture, furniture, fixtures and fittings. This was repeated at several Wirral stations the same year and would doubtless have been used at the new Euston but for the intervention of WW2.

It's said that little things please little minds and when I started commuting to London I was delighted to see a flickering neon sign on the McVitie's biscuit factory at Willesden which, complete with directional arrow, proclaimed that it was '15 minutes to Euston'. Again, when as a St. Rollox engineering apprentice I started travelling to and from Glasgow, I was grat-

Apsley in LMS days with its 'Hawkseye' pattern nameboards, introduced in the same year as the station's construction. The signs were made up of minute spheres of coloured glass, off-white for the background and yellow with black lettering for the title. These, being free from dazzle, were equally legible under artificial light as in daylight as well as being easy to clean. BR rather spoiled the effect by painting the whole thing maroon and picking out the totem and lettering in white.
COLLECTION R. M. CASSERLEY

The cover of the John Dickinson Ltd. house magazine recording the opening of Apsley station.

ified to see a sign painted on a wall just south of Atherstone reading '102 miles to London'.

When I eventually became a Building Services Engineer with the Chief Civil Engineer's Department at Euston in 1956, regular region-wide travel became commonplace, as often as two or three times a week, especially in the last ten years as the Maintenance & Renewal Assistant. From Bangor to Barrow, Croxley to Carlisle, Derby to Dublin, Northampton to Newton Heath, St. Albans to St. Helens,

Walsall to Workington, I roamed the length and breadth of the LMR and beyond. When the former GWR Birmingham and Wolverhampton Districts were taken over in the early sixties, I discovered just how long it took to get to Aberystwyth and back. These days as I make less frequent rail trips 'North of Watford', I look out for buildings and other works in which I was involved, to bring back memories and to see if they are still functioning or, indeed, even still exist. A long rectangle of weed and scrub-

Recently destreamlined (January 1947) Stanier Pacific 6237 City of Bristol passing the Ovaltine factory underneath King's Langley's outer home on an up express. Just behind the photographer was underbridge No. 73 giving vehicular access to the egg farm and goods yard. Rail access to the latter was controlled by a ground frame, electrically released from King's Langley signal box over a quarter of a mile away on the other side of the station.
C. R. L. COLES

A 1930s poster depicting the Ovaltine Egg and Dairy Farms, the latter home to a renowned herd of pedigree Jersey cattle. A modern version of the Ovaltine dairymaid still appears on their products.

The Ovaltine factory in the 1950s. When I eventually cycled to and from school, the return journey was timed as ten minutes to the Apsley Mills clock, which had 'BASILDON BOND' spelt around its face instead of numbers, a further ten minutes to the Ovaltine clock and another ten minutes up home to Abbots Langley.
AUTHOR'S COLLECTION

strewn wasteland with a broken two foot high boundary wall is all that remains of Monument Lane Carriage Shed for example. Again, in 1969 a new repair shop for Merry-go-round Wagons was erected at Burton-on-Trent. It's now fenced off and in private hands yet the nearby, much larger building continues to advertise its railway heritage, albeit in fading lettering: 'MIDLAND RAILWAY BONDED STORE & GRAIN WAREHOUSE No. 4'. I'm pleased to say that the smaller No. 2 building at the station proudly announces its antiquity in new black and white paint.

As mentioned earlier, throughout these wanderings two sites have remained places of particular pleasure. The first, near to home, is the Ovaltine factory at King's Langley erected by A. Wander Ltd in the late twenties. In the LMS film *Coronation Scot* the test run was photographed from a tracking aircraft and the sequence begins as the train powers past the factory. The archaic commentary has it that 'the run provided such an orgy of speed as never before indulged in over LMS metals' and concludes, 'A supreme effort and *Coronation* has done it. 114 miles an hour, the highest speed yet attained in the Empire.' One of the principal commodities handled in the adjacent King's Langley goods yard was sacked wheat for the factory. In my school days I normally caught the 8.21 from the station but sometimes managed the earlier 7.57, known, as I later discovered, by the Willesden men who worked it as 'The Tring Flyer'. Intending passengers for the latter had to be on the platform before it drew in, otherwise they were swept back down the subway stairs by the flood of Ovaltine workers who then marched off down Station Road in a chattering crocodile. In those days the hillside from Abbots Langley down into the Gade Valley was covered in up to 100,000 white leghorn chickens, now sadly all gone and the land rent asunder by a cutting to carry the M25. In 2002 the company moved its business back to Switzerland but the factory's 387ft long, five-storey, art deco façade has been saved by an enlightened planning authority/developer. Behind it, instead of a busy factory, the world's largest producer of malt extract used extensively in the food industry, there is a residential complex of over 200 homes. I feel obliged to confess some personal connections in that, not only was I an Ovaltiney, one of those 'happy girls and boys', but my mother was the factory's

canteen Manageress during the war and my sister retired as Personnel Manager.

So 172 miles further in the 'frozen north' as my Crewe Divisional Services Supervisor used to say, lies Wigan. On the up side beyond the North Western station just past the low-level L&Y Wallgate Station, is a large building whose gable end, facing the railway, is emblazoned with the cheeful message: 'UNCLE JOE'S MINT BALLS KEEP YOU ALL AGLOW'. This is the Dorning Street factory of William Santus & Co. Ltd built in 1919 although the company was established elsewhere in 1899. The first mint ball was produced in 1921 and was officially patented in 1933. The only ingredients are peppermint, specially imported from America, sugar and cream of tartar and the exact recipe is known only to the current Managing Directors. The reason that they turn to a dark sticky candy is because there are no chemical colourings and preservatives. These days they are wrapped and sold in 200g (7.05oz) tins – there's a half empty one on my desk as I write. At one time, however, they could be purchased individually and unwrapped, which leads me into the tale told by Michael Burke in *Signalman* (Bradford Barton). He had started as a signal box lad at Miles Platting in 1953 but at the time in question he was a signalman at Phillips Park No. 2..

'That stalwart of signalling staff, the signal lineman, usually visited us on the early turn of duty. The man responsible for all things mechanical at this box revelled in the curious nickname of 'Uncle Joe' because of his addiction to a sweet of the same name. His real name, which no one ever used, was Freddy Boydell. These sweets were kept in a congealed mess in one of his overall pockets, along with bits of oily waste, nuts, bolts and the like. He was a generous soul and insisted on handing over one of these so-called sweets each time he saw you, which was about six times a shift on the day he visited us. I quite like toffees normally but these were not only terrifically hot but always flavoured with signal oil and garnished with fluff. I liked Freddy despite all this because he was such a nice person and would do anything for you; his only problem was that he seemed to be naturally accident prone.

'One incident involving him concerned our Up Main Line Home Signal which was an upper quadrant some 180 yards from the box. Lever No. 3 pulled this and the action was so smooth that the signal would fly up, almost turning turtle before dropping back to the correct 60 degree angle. I felt that it should even be possible to turn the signal arm right over until I realised that arms were fitted with a device to prevent this happening, probably due to the constant hammering being given to it by our 'heave-ho' methods, one day the bracket snapped and I saw the signal arm go sailing over the top of its arc to finish up in the back to front position. This was evidently to the consternation of the driver of an

The Santus factory in Dorning Street, Wigan, which opened in 1919. The business started with a market stall in 1898 with treacle toffee as a speciality made by the founder's wife in her kitchen. Eventually a small domestic factory was built in the shadow of the huge Rylands Cotton Mill but demand for the products forced the move to the present premises. Today's citizens of Wigan are able to purchase them at Uncle Joe's Emporium, Crompton Street.

A 1930s Wm. Santus & Co. advertisement: Uncle Joe's Mint Balls – handy for the pocket.

approaching freight who yanked the whistle vigorously on his Black Five, but kept going as he could see the starter and distant ahead were all in the 'all clear' position.

'With this damage done, I now had to call Freddy to come and put things back to normal. When he arrived and saw what I had done to one of his signals, he called me all the names he could think of, whilst those names he forgot his mate made use of! The signal arm, it was decided, would have to be disconnected and Freddy left the box in order to trace the signal wire through the run. I should add that all signal wires run collectively over pulleys mounted in metal or wooden frames, the expanse of wire stretching from the lever to the signal being known as the 'run'. He was bending over straddling the run and tracing the wire by the usual method of pulling each in turn until he found the one that lifted the counterbalance weight on the signal he was after.

'I carried on working normally until I pulled the Up Goods Outer Home Signal, Lever No. 6, which, being some 350 yards from the box, required a big hefty pull. This was so that I could draw a Castleton–Belle Vue special freight alongside the water column and then up to the Inner Home Signal for it to pin down wagon brakes. As I did so, I heard a sudden shout and a string of curses. I ran to the box window, to find that Freddy was lying entangled with his legs in the air amongst the signal wires, swearing like anything at the top of his voice. It transpired that he had grabbed the wire to signal No. 6 at the same time that I pulled it and this had turned him over as neatly as any Judo expert could have done it. Freddy's assistant, who was up in the box with me, had to be hurriedly asked to leave his priority duties, namely the production of hot tea, to come outside and help extricate his mate. After brushing Freddy down and restoring his dignity a little, they managed to get the job done and the signal repaired. I knew that all was forgiven when they were departing and Freddy said, "Well, Burky, we'll be off now. Have an Uncle Joe's", and was handed a fluff-covered sweet.'

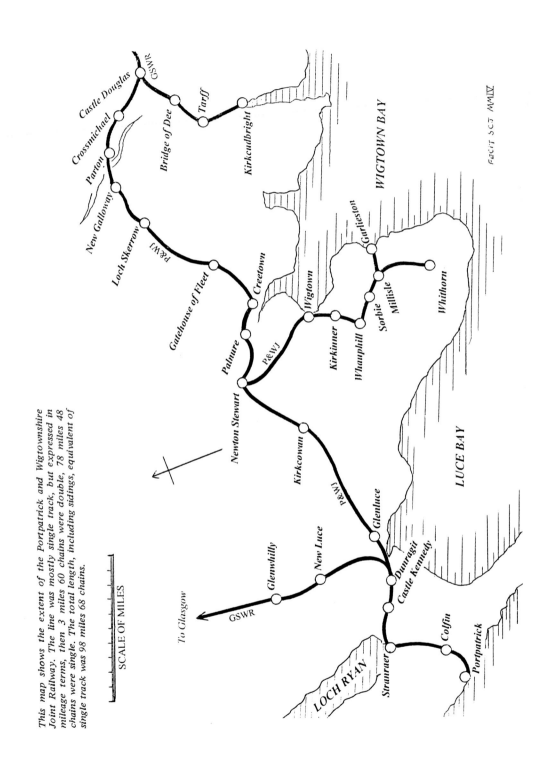

This map shows the extent of the Portpatrick and Wigtownshire Joint Railway. The line was mostly single track, but expressed in mileage terms, then 3 miles 60 chains were double, 78 miles 48 chains were single. The total length, including sidings, equivalent of single track was 98 miles 68 chains.

SCALE OF MILES

To Glasgow

GSWR

LOCH RYAN

Stranraer

Colfin

Portpatrick

Dunragit

Castle Kennedy

Glenwhilly

New Luce

Glenluce

P&WJ

Kirkcowan

Newton Stewart

Palnure

Creetown

Gatehouse of Fleet

Loch Skerron

New Galloway

Parton

Crossmichael

Castle Douglas

GSWR

Bridge of Dee

Tarff

Kirkcudbright

WIGTOWN BAY

LUCE BAY

P&WJ

Wigtown

Kirkinner

Whauphill

Sorbie

Millisle

Gurlieston

Whithorn

FECIT SCJ MMIV

The Portpatrick & Wigtownshire Joint Line

by STANLEY C. JENKINS MA

An Edwardian scene at Newton Stewart. The Whithorn branch train had evidently just arrived and travellers were awaiting the arrival of an up train to Dumfries. LENS OF SUTTON COLLECTION

THE south-western lowlands of Scotland are rarely visited by tourists or holiday-makers, who usually head for more famous tourist destinations such as the Highlands or Western Isles. For railway enthusiasts, however, the former counties of Kirkcudbrightshire and Wigtownshire are of particular interest in that they were served by one of Britain's most extensive joint systems – the Portpatrick & Wigtownshire Railways Joint Committee. The P&WJ was co-owned by no less than four Pregrouping companies: the Caledonian Railway, the Glasgow & South Western Railway, the Midland Railway and the London & North Western Railway. It was predominantly single track, and served the ferry port to Ireland at Stranraer.

THE RAILWAY MANIA IN SOUTH-WESTERN SCOTLAND

Scottish railways developed independently of the English system and, by the start of the 'Railway Mania', there was already an extensive network of lines in the populous industrial districts around Glasgow and Edinburgh. Subsequent developments were concerned with the provision of main-line links between England and Scotland, the Caledonian Railway being incorporated by Act of Parliament on 31st July 1845 to form a northwards continua-

tion of what today is called the West Coast Main Line from London, while the rival North British Railway was sanctioned on 4th July 1844, with powers for the construction of a line between Edinburgh and Berwick-upon-Tweed.

Although the creation of a main-line rail network during the 1840s was a triumph of private enterprise, the British government exercised considerable control over the new railways. Official policy had encouraged the building of these Anglo-Scottish trunk routes while, at the same time, the government was keen to support the creation of similar main-line links between Ireland and the British mainland. The 'United Kingdom of Great Britain & Ireland' was barely forty years old by the 1840s, and it was felt that the construction of viable Anglo-Irish rail and steamer routes would help to forge the disparate parts of the country into a prosperous and fully unified British nation.

There were, accordingly, several early proposals for a rail link between Carlisle and the long-established Post Office packet station at Portpatrick. The aptly-named 'British & Irish Union Railway', for example, was promoted during the Railway Mania with the aim of building a line to Portpatrick. Unfortunately, a series of harvest failures in the mid to late 1840s

led to a severe economic crisis and a total collapse in business confidence. In parts of Ireland, poorer people were, quite literally, starving to death while, even in England, the labouring classes were facing destitution.

In these melancholy circumstances, many of the grandiose railway schemes concocted during the Railway Mania were abandoned in their entirety. Others were brought to completion and, by the early 1850s, the main-line railway network in south-western Scotland had reached its present form. The Caledonian Railway forged northwards from Carlisle to Glasgow while, further to the west, the Glasgow & South Western route formed an alternative path for long-distance traffic via Annan, Dumfries and the Nith Valley.

THE CASTLE DOUGLAS & DUMFRIES RAILWAY

The completion of the Glasgow & South Western main line in 1850 was a source of obvious encouragement for the residents of small towns such as Kirkcudbright and Castle Douglas, who were keen to see the creation of a direct rail link between Dumfries, Castle Douglas and Kirkcudbright. Such a line had first been suggested during the Railway Mania, but no real progress was made until the early 1850s, when the G&SWR started to take a benign interest in a local company known as the Castle Douglas & Dumfries Railway, which had been sanctioned by Parliament on 21st July 1856 (19 & 20 Vic.cap.114).

Construction of the Dumfries to Castle Douglas line was started in March 1857 and the railway was ready for goods traffic by October 1859. However, following a dispute, the junction at Dumfries was blocked by the contractors. In an attempt to end the impasse, the railway company was obliged to apply for an interdict (injunction), and when this was granted, the line was opened for goods traffic. Finally, on 7th November 1859, the railway was opened throughout between Dumfries and Castle Douglas, a distance of 19 miles 55 chains.

On 1st August 1861, the Kirkcudbright Railway was sanctioned by Parliament as a 10¼ mile extension of the Castle Douglas & Dumfries line. The first sod was ceremonially cut at Kirkcudbright on 30th June 1862, and construction of the single-track branch was soon under way. Goods traffic commenced between Castle Douglas and Kirkcudbright on 17th February 1864, but the Board of Trade refused to sanction the use of the junction at Castle Douglas by passenger trains until the track layout had been modified.

In order to overcome this unexpected problem, it was agreed that a passenger service would be arranged between Kirkcudbright and a temporary station at Castle Douglas. Having reached this compromise solution, the Kirkcudbright Railway was opened for passenger traffic on 7th March 1864, the northern terminus of the branch being in St. Andrew Street, Castle Douglas. Passenger trains were allowed to run to and from the main-line station with effect from 15th August 1864, although the St. Andrew Street station was not officially closed until 1st December 1867.

The Castle Douglas & Dumfries Railway and the Kirkcudbright branch were, from their inception, worked by the Glasgow & South Western Railway. This situation continued until 1865, when both companies were amalgamated with the G&SWR company. In the meantime, plans were underway for the construction of the long hoped-for Anglo-Irish main line, which would in effect continue the Castle Douglas route westwards to Portpatrick and Stranraer.

THE PORTPATRICK RAILWAY

The cross-channel route between Portpatrick and Northern Ireland was of considerable antiquity, regular services having been introduced as long ago as the 17th century. The distance between Portpatrick and Donaghadee in County Down is only 22 miles, Ulster being clearly visible from the cliffs around Portpatrick. Steamers had appeared on this 'short sea' route in 1837, when the *Dasher* and *Arrow* were used to carry government mails. Later, the Admiralty vessels *Fury* and *Spitfire*

were employed, and in 1850 Portpatrick harbour was taken over by the government.

In the mid-1850s, a group of public-spirited local gentlemen decided to form a railway company with the aim of securing a rail link between Portpatrick and the Castle Douglas & Dumfries Railway at Castle Douglas, the necessary parliamentary Bill being submitted in time for the 1857 session. This ambitious scheme was, in effect, the lineal descendant of the British & Irish Union Railway and other abortive projects that had been suggested during the Railway Mania years of the 1840s.

The Portpatrick Railway Company was incorporated by Act of Parliament on 10th August 1857 (20 & 21 Vic.cap.149) with powers for the construction of a line extending from Castle Douglas to Portpatrick. The authorised route was via Parton, Newton Stewart and Stranraer, a distance of a little over sixty miles. There would, in addition, be short branches at Stranraer and Portpatrick, the Stranraer branch diverging from the main line in the parish of Inch and terminating near Stranraer harbour, a distance of 70 chains, while the Portpatrick branch would run from Portpatrick station to the pier on the north side of Portpatrick Harbour, a distance of 40 chains.

To pay for their scheme, the promoters were authorised to raise a total of £460,000 in ten pound shares, together with a further £150,000 by loans. The Lancaster & Carlisle and Glasgow & South Western companies agreed to subscribe a combined total of £200,000, whilst the Belfast & County Down Railway would contribute the more modest sum of £15,000. In return for their support, these three companies were allowed to appoint directors to the Portpatrick Railway board, which would consist of ten 'local' directors, together with two Lancaster & Carlisle representatives, two from the Glasgow & South Western company and one from the Belfast & County Down Railway.

The principal supporters included prominent local landowners and gentlemen such as Lord Stair of Culorn, Sir William Dunbar MP of Mertonhall, Sir Andrew Agnew MP of Lochnaw, Sir John McTaggart of Ardwell, Colonel James McDougal of Logan, Sir John C. D. Hay of Park Place, Horatio G.M.Stewart of Gatehouse, John Moore of Coursewall, and Wellwood Maxwell of Glenlee. Collectively, these individuals represented the cream of local society. They were joined, as directors of the company, by William N. Hodgson MP of Newby Grange and Lieutenant-Colonel H. D. Maclean of Penrith, representing the Lancaster & Carlisle Railway, and representatives from the Glasgow & South Western and Belfast & County Down railways.

Construction began in 1858 and, despite the magnitude of their task, the railway builders made commendable progress, the railway being ceremonially opened between Castle Douglas and Stranraer on Monday, 11th March 1861.

Work was, by this time, under way on the final section between Stranraer and Portpatrick, and in March 1862 *The Galloway Advertiser & Wigtownshire Free Press* reported that Portpatrick station and the associated harbour branch had been completed, although about seventy men were still hard at work in the new basin.

The Stranraer to Portpatrick line was opened on 28th August 1862. As usual in those days, Opening Day was treated as a great public holiday, the first train being greeted by deafening cheers, while the Portpatrick Artillery Volunteers fired a thunderous salute from their recently-completed coast defence battery. At 11.30 am the steamer *Heroine* arrived, carrying over six hundred excursionists, who had sailed from Donaghadee to celebrate the great occasion; many of these Irish visitors walked up to the passenger station, from where a special train conveyed them to and from Stranraer.

With their railway completed throughout to its western terminus at Portpatrick, the directors anticipated that traffic would rapidly increase. The report for the half-year ending 31st January 1862 showed that receipts had amounted to £7,627, leaving a surplus of £1,439 after the payment of debentures and all other expenses. Similarly, the revenue account for the half-year ending 31st July 1862 revealed that £7,712 had been received and £5,424 expended, leaving a balance of £2,288 which, when added to £4,131 from previous years, made £6,419; after interest and other payments had been deducted, this left a cumulative balance of £4,313.

These results seemed, at first glance, to have been relatively encouraging, but in practice the Portpatrick Railway directors were becoming gravely concerned about the future of the steamer route to Donaghadee. In September 1862 they reported that:

'If the government had shown sufficient energy in pushing on the works for the improvement of the harbour, the company would now be reaping the full benefit of their connection with the short sea passage to Ireland.

'Little progress had been made on the harbour works, and the directors had consequently addressed a memorial to the Admiralty, urging, in the strongest terms, the obligations which the government undertook to have the works concluded as soon as this company should be in a condition to use it in connection with their line.

'In the meanwhile, and with the special object of bringing Irish traffic over the line, the directors, taking advantage of the opening of the railway from Belfast to Larne, have, in conjunction with the Northern Counties of Ireland, the Castle Douglas & Dumfries and the London & North Western, entered into an arrangement for establishing a daily passage between Stranraer and Larne, which they hope will be the means of adding greatly to the traffic on the railway'.

Sadly, the Portpatrick to Donaghadee steamer service was not a success. This was, in part, because the station at Portpatrick was poorly sited in relation to the steamer piers, whilst the harbour branch was steeply-graded and difficult to work. However, on 1st October 1862, the Portpatrick Railway had opened its branch from Stranraer to Stranraer Harbour, in the sheltered waters of Loch Ryan. The steamer service between Stranraer and Larne was an instant success, and this sealed the fate of the Stranraer to Portpatrick line, which became a purely local route from Stranraer. The Portpatrick Harbour branch was lifted in 1875, after every attempt to revive the Donaghadee steamer route had failed.

The Portpatrick Railway had initially worked its own train services, but on 29th July 1864 the company obtained a new Act of Parliament (27 & 28 Vic.cap.317), authorising an additional £20,000 in shares and £20,000 by loan, and permitting the local company to enter into working arrangements with the Caledonian and London & North Western railways. A separate Act (27 & 28 Vic.cap.318), passed on the same day, permitted the Portpatrick Railway Company to establish its own cross-channel steamer services between Portpatrick and Donaghadee, and between Stranraer and Larne, for which purpose a further £72,000 in shares and £24,000 by loans was authorised.

In 1864, the Portpatrick directors signed an agreement with the Caledonian Railway whereby that company would work the line for a period of twenty-one years, commencing on 1st October 1864, at a maximum rate of 38 per cent of the gross receipts, falling to 33 per cent as the traffic increased. At the same time, the Portpatrick Railway's locomotives, rolling stock and workshop equipment were 'disposed of to the Caledonian Railway on advantageous terms, and from the funds thus realised, and from the price of 1,000 additional ordinary shares taken up by the London & North Western Railway', the directors were able to pay off £30,000 of the debenture debt.

The capital account for the half-year ending 31st July 1865 reveals that the Portpatrick Railway had received £556,500 in shares, debentures and interest, while expenditure had included £53,315 on 'land and compensation', £462,494 on 'works', £13,826 on engineering expenses, £45,566 on rolling stock, £6,360 on legal and Parliamentary expenses and £3,375 on management, advertising postage and other sundry expenses. The revenue account had shown a moderate increase over the corresponding period for 1864, and from the balance of £3,107 which remained after payment of debenture interest and other expenses, a dividend of one per cent per annum was declared on the ordinary shares.

In presenting their report to the proprietors, the Portpatrick Railway directors congratulated the shareholders 'on the prospect of at length obtaining some return on the capital' that had been invested in the undertaking. The 'working agreement with the Caledonian Railway' had, they added, 'been carried out in a liberal and enterprising spirit, and its beneficial effects were already apparent'. In 1868, the company received an unexpected windfall when the Treasury agreed to pay £20,000 in compensation following the government's decision to withdraw its support for the Portpatrick to Donaghadee ferry!

Conversely, the Stranraer to Larne service was going from strength to strength, aided by the interest shown by large railway companies such as the London & Western Railway and its Caledonian partner. By 1872, the 497 ton paddle steamer *Princess Louise* had been placed in service on the route, followed by the larger, 556 ton PS *Princess Beatrice* in 1875 and the 1,096 ton PS *Princess Victoria*, which was added to the fleet in 1890.

In retrospect, the success of the ferry service between Stranraer and Larne more than made up for the failure of the Portpatrick route, the still-flourishing faculties at Stranraer Harbour being a tangible reminder of the vision and energy of Victorian gentlemen such as the Earl of Stair and Sir William Dunbar.

THE WIGTOWNSHIRE RAILWAY

The Portpatrick Railway served a large rural area, but there were persistent demands for a branch line to be built southwards from the Portpatrick route to serve the prosperous agricultural district around Wigtown. The first proposals for a line from Newton Stewart to Wigtown, Sorbie and Whithorn were made in the 1860s, but the sudden failure of bankers Overend & Gurney in May 1866 made it increasingly difficult for the promoters of small companies to raise the necessary capital, and the scheme remained dormant for several years.

The Wigtownshire project was revived in 1871, when a new company was formed by local landowners and entrepreneurs who were keen to see the obvious advantages of rail transport brought to Wigtown and the Machars peninsula. The necessary Act of Parliament was obtained on 18th July 1872, when the Wigtownshire Railway Company was incorporated with powers for the construction and maintenance of a railway commencing at Newton Stewart by a junction with the Portpatrick Railway and terminating in Whithorn. A contract for construction of the line was awarded to John Granger of Aberdeen, and work was under way by the summer of 1873.

The authorised route traversed low-lying terrain, and with few physical obstacles to hinder the work rapid progress was made. The new railway was ready for opening between Newton Stewart and Wigtown by the summer of 1874, but no arrangements had been made for working the line. It was at first suggested that the branch might be worked by the Caledonian Railway, but in practice it was impossible for the Caledonian and Wigtownshire companies to make an amicable working agreement. An impasse having arisen,

John Granger put the Wigtownshire directors into contact with Thomas Wheatley (1821–1883), who had recently been forced to resign as Locomotive Superintendent of the North British Railway.

Helped by his son, Thomas Wheatley obtained two small locomotives and an assortment of elderly passenger vehicles, and by this means it was possible for the line to be opened between Newton Stewart and Wigtown on 5th April 1875. On 2nd August 1875 the line was extended from Wigtown to Millisle (then called Garlieston), and in 1876 the route was further extended to Garlieston Harbour. Finally, on 9th July 1877, the Wigtownshire Railway was opened throughout to its southern terminus at Whithorn. The completed railway was a 19 mile single-track route, with a short branch from Millisle to Garlieston Harbour. The most significant engineering work was the River Bladnoch Viaduct near Wigtown.

The Wheatleys operated the Wigtownshire Railway with a small fleet of locomotives and rolling stock, the first engine obtained for service on the line being a 2–2–2 well tank that had been built for use on the Peebles to Hawick line in 1856; the engine was subsequently reconstructed as a 2–4–0. The next engine acquired was an 0–4–2 that had been rebuilt as a tank engine in 1870, while Wigtownshire Railway No. 3 was an 0–4–2T named *Addison*. Engine No. 4 was a small Beyer Peacock tank engine named *Gardner* which was converted into a tender engine on its arrival at Wigtown. Locomotive No. 5 was a diminutive 2–2–2 well tank, and finally No. 6 was a Manning Wardle 0–6–0ST.

THE PORTPATRICK & WIGTOWNSHIRE JOINT COMMITTEE

The Portpatrick Railway had been built to provide through communication between Scotland and Ireland, and although early plans for a steamer service between Portpatrick and Donaghadee were soon abandoned, the alternative route from Stranraer to Larne was highly successful. It was undoubtedly the growing importance of this steamer service that attracted the Midland and London & North Western railways into the area, although it should be remembered that the LNWR and G&SWR companies had been associated with the Portpatrick Railway from its very inception.

The involvement of the Midland Railway was, at first glance, more of a surprise, though in practice the MR had been interested in the provision of Anglo-Irish steamer services for several years, the company being a co-owner of the Barrow Steam Navigation Company, which had been formed in 1867 to run cross-channel services between Morecambe and Belfast. The Midland was, moreover, a close ally of the G&SWR, and in these circumstances the Midland's actions can be more readily understood.

In 1885, following a series of negotiations, it was agreed that the Portpatrick and Wigtownshire railways would be purchased by an alliance of the Midland, Glasgow & South Western, Caledonian and London & North Western companies. The new concern would be known as The Portpatrick & Wigtownshire Joint Railways.

These new arrangements were formalised by an Act of Parliament obtained on 6th August 1885, which merged the Portpatrick and Wigtownshire railways and vested them in the new undertaking. Although the P&WJ system was jointly owned by the Caledonian, G&SWR, Midland and LNWR companies, the P&WJR was regarded as a legal entity in its own right, and it had many of the attributes of an independent company. For example, the railway issued its own tickets, while Joint Committee staff wore distinctive uniforms to differentiate them from ordinary G&SWR or Caledonian employees.

The Portpatrick & Wigtownshire Railways Joint Committee worked a system of 81 miles and, as such, it was one of the largest joint lines in the country. The P&WJ was worked by rolling stock from all four owning companies, though only Scottish locomotives appeared on the line prior to the 1923 Grouping. The P&WJ system included two branches, one of which was the former main line between Stranraer and Portpatrick, while the other was the Wigtownshire route from Newton Stewart to Whithorn. The Kirkcudbright line, which left the Stranraer route at Castle Douglas, was worked exclusively by G&SWR locomotives and rolling stock.

Joint ownership came to an end in 1923, when the Portpatrick & Wigtownshire Joint line passed into LMS control under the provisions of the Railways Act of 1921. Thereafter, the railways in this south-western extremity of Scotland became part of a homogeneous system – though it is interesting to note that stocks of Portpatrick & Wigtownshire tickets were available for many years after the Grouping.

THE IRISH TUNNEL SCHEME

There were, from time to time, suggestions that a tunnel might be constructed between Scotland and Ireland. At a time when Irish 'Home Rule' was dominating political debate, the provision of a physical link between Ireland and the British mainland would have sent out a powerful anti-Home Rule message. As an engineering operation, the Irish Tunnel idea was perfectly feasible, and in the 1890s it seemed possible that the scheme would be implemented. On 27th October 1890, for instance, *The Oxfordshire Weekly News* printed the following progress report:

'The proposed Irish Channel Tunnel is now so far advanced that the Mayor of Belfast has convened a meeting to consider the scheme. A requisition, signed by about seventy representative men of the North of Ireland, states their belief that the tunnel to connect the Antrim coast with the coast of Wigtownshire, and thereby the railway systems of Scotland and England with Belfast and the North of Ireland, would be a great public advantage.'

If the suggested tunnel had even been built it would have had profound implications for the P&WJ route, and for the Belfast & Northern Counties Railway – which would presumably have been narrowed from 5ft 3in gauge to standard gauge to facilitate through running from the mainland system. In the event, the 1912 Home Rule crisis probably dealt a final blow to the Irish tunnel scheme, though the Portpatrick & Wigtownshire and Belfast & Northern Counties companies were brought into closer association on 1st July 1903, when the B&NR was absorbed by the Midland Railway.

THE LINE IN OPERATION

The earliest timetables provided three through trains each way between Castle Douglas and Stranraer, the service being extended to Portpatrick in 1862. At that time the Portpatrick route was the only rail outlet for steamer traffic from Portpatrick or Stranraer but, on 5th October 1877, the completion of the Girvan & Portpatrick Railway provided an alternative route for traffic passing between Belfast and Glasgow. The Girvan route joined the Portpatrick line at Challoch Junction, between Dunragit and Castle Kennedy, but it did not detract from the importance of the earlier route via Castle Douglas, which continued to carry passenger and freight traffic between England and Northern Ireland.

At the end of the Victorian period, the basic timetable provided half-a-dozen trains each way between Dumfries and Stranraer. In 1904, for instance, there were six up and five down workings between Stranraer and Dumfries. In the up direction, the main eastbound through services left Stranraer at 7.35 am, 9.30 pm, 12.30 pm, 3.40 pm, 6.50 pm and 9.08 pm, while balancing down workings departed from Dumfries at 3.55 am, 8.50 am, 2.50 pm, 5.27 pm and 8.00 pm.

Some of these workings were limited-stop services that omitted most of the smaller intermediate stopping places on the Portpatrick & Wigtownshire Joint line. The most important service was the Belfast boat train, which generally left Carlisle at 3.10 am and arrived at Stranraer Harbour at 5.47 am, having called intermediately at Dumfries, Castle Douglas and Newton Stewart. This prestigious service conveyed through sleeping cars from the West Coast and Midland routes, which had left Euston and St Pancras at 8.00 pm and 8.30 pm respectively on the previous evening.

In the reverse direction, the balancing up service left Stranraer Harbour at 9.08 pm, and having called en route at Newton Stewart at 9.45 pm and Castle Douglas at 10.32 pm, the boat train continued to Carlisle. The separate London portions then went on their separate ways, the Midland sleeping cars reaching St. Pancras by 7.10 am, while the London & North Western through coaches arrived at Euston at 7.35 am. It is perhaps surprising that this important main-line service should have stopped at both Newton Stewart and Castle Douglas – though it may be significant that both of these stations were junctions, at which branch lines joined the main P&WJ route between Dumfries and Stranraer.

Train services on the Whithorn branch were modest in the extreme, and at no time in its history did this remote line ever support more than half-a-dozen trains each way. In the early days, the line was worked by four passenger trains in each direction, together with one goods working, while at the end of the Victorian period the normal timetable provided four up and five down passenger trains, with an extra down service on Fridays only; there were no Sunday services. The unbalanced distribution of up and down workings probably reflected a pattern of operation whereby the engine that arrived at Whithorn with the second train of the day later returned to Newton Stewart with an up goods working.

The ending of joint ownership as a result of the 1923 Grouping made little difference to the pattern of operations on the P&WJ line. The 1923 public timetable provided five up and six down workings between Stranraer and Dumfries, with up services from Stranraer at 7.35 am, 9.30 am, 12.15 pm, 3.40 pm and 9.42, and down services from Dumfries at 3.40 am, 4.05 am, 8.35 am, 2.38 pm, 5.30pm and 7.37 pm.

The Kirkcudbright branch was served by seven up and nine down workings, many of which ran to or from Dumfries, giving a number of additional workings for Castle Douglas travellers. At the western end of the P&WJ route, the Portpatrick branch was served by six trains each way, whilst the Whithorn branch service comprised four up and five down workings, with an extra train in each direction on Fridays.

In addition to its scheduled main-line and branch-line services, the Portpatrick & Wigtownshire Joint line carried a certain amount of special traffic in the form of troop trains and summer excursions. As far as military traffic was concerned, the line from Dumfries to Stranraer became particularly important after the 26 counties of Southern Ireland succeeded from the United Kingdom in 1921, leaving just six predominantly Protestant counties within the UK. This development meant that the Holyhead to Dublin and Fishguard to Rosslare ferry routes could no longer be used for military purposes – leaving the Stranraer to Larne service as the principal ferry link used by British military personnel.

The strategic importance of the Stranraer route was even greater during World War Two, when it was feared that the Germans would attempt to secure a foothold in Southern Ireland – from where they could attack

Stranraer Harbour station, looking south from the seaward end of the pier. There were two stations at Stranraer, the Harbour station at the end of a short branch line, and Stranraer, which was on the through line to Portpatrick. Stranraer Harbour station was opened on 1st October 1862, and Stranraer was opened on 12th March 1861, but renamed Stranraer Town by BR on 2nd March 1953. It was closed on 7th March 1966. The total length of the platforms at Stranraer Harbour station was 1,226 feet, whilst at Stranraer it was 1,524 feet. The two-funnelled steamer visible alongside the jetty appears to have been the Princess Maud, *launched in 1904, 300ft overall and with a gross tonnage of 1,655 tons. Hulls were black and funnels buff-coloured.*   LENS OF SUTTON COLLECTION

A postcard view showing the rear of the up side station building at New Galloway, c.1912. Motor vehicles and horse transport were awaiting the arrival of the next train.   LENS OF SUTTON COLLECTION

Newton Stewart station in Victorian days. A Stirling 0–4–2, with its characteristic domeless boiler, had just arrived with an up working to Dumfries.

LENS OF SUTTON COLLECTION

Northern Ireland or the British mainland. To reduce this threat, the Northern Irish garrison was heavily-reinforced, large numbers of troop trains being sent along the P&WJ route to Stranraer, while other military traffic was routed via Ayr and Girvan. Figures released after the war revealed that no less than 5,059,625 passengers had used the Stranraer ferry route between 1939 and 1945, 4,305,922 of these journeys being made by service personnel.

Other important wartime traffic routed via the P&WJ line during World War Two included Churchill tanks that had been built by Harland & Wolff in Belfast, and were sent to mainland Britain via Larne Harbour. In 1941, work began on the construction of an emergency harbour at Cairnryan, to the north-east of Stranraer. This wartime project brought constructional traffic to the P&WJ route although, when opened in March 1943, the completed harbour was essentially an emergency military port, and it was never fully-utilised (see below).

After World War Two, the Dumfries to Stranraer service settled down to a basic pattern of four trains each way. In July 1947, the up workings departed from Stranraer at 8.00 a.m., 12.35 p.m., 3.30 p.m. and 10.00 p.m., whilst down trains left Dumfries at 2.00 a.m., 3.55 a.m., 8.40 a.m. and 6.10 p.m. An extra boat train was provided on Fridays and Saturdays, the up service leaving Stranraer Harbour at 12.35 p.m., whilst the down working left Dumfries at 2.42 p.m. and arrived at Stranraer Harbour at 5.12 p.m. The Kirkcudbright branch was served by six up and seven down workings, whilst the Whithorn route had three

up and four down services; services on the Portpatrick branch had decreased to just two trains each way.

On 1st January 1948 the main-line railway companies were nationalised as part of a unified transport organisation known as British Railways, though in practice there were few obvious changes on the Portpatrick & Wigtownshire system, which continued to be served by four through trains in each direction. In the mid-1950s, the first down service to leave Dumfries was the 4.00 a.m. boat train, which conveyed through sleeping cars from London Euston, and had been dubbed the 'Northern Irishman' on 30th June 1952. The next down workings were the 6.35 a.m. and 8.10 a.m. branch trains to Kirkcudbright, followed by the 8.45 a.m. service to Stranraer. Operations continued with further departures for Stranraer at 2.50 p.m. and 6.30 p.m., and a local train to Kirkcudbright at 6.02 p.m. The corresponding eastbound services left Stranraer at 8.05 a.m., 10.58 a.m., 3.40 p.m. and 10.00 p.m., the latter service being the up 'Northern Irishman', which reached Euston at 8.10 a.m. on the following morning.

Study of these timings will reveal that the train service offered to the travelling public had never been particularly convenient. The long-distance boat trains were timed to connect with sailings on the Stranraer to Larne ferry route, and they were of little use to people trying to reach Dumfries or Stranraer for work or shopping. The Kirkcudbright through workings did, it is true, provide some additional workings at the east end of the line, but there was still a huge gap in the middle of the day when no services were available. At a time when

increasing numbers of people were investing in private motor vehicles, it appeared that BR was unwilling to arrange a realistic local train service.

MOTIVE POWER

The Portpatrick & Wigtownshire Joint line may not have been a particularly busy route by main-line standards, but it was, over the years, worked by a variety of different locomotive classes. In its independent days, this lengthy cross-country route was worked by a small fleet of mainly Sharp Stewart locomotives, which probably resembled the standard 'Sharpies' supplied to many other railway companies during the mid-Victorian period. Later, following the Caledonian takeover, passenger trains were typically hauled by Conner 2–4–0s, whilst goods traffic was handled by Caledonian 0–4–2s.

Throughout this period, G&SWR locomotives had been familiar sights between Castle Douglas and Dumfries, and on the Kirkcudbright branch, this part of the Dumfries to Stranraer route being purely Glasgow & South Western property. As a result of the 1885 agreement, G&SWR locomotives began to work through to the P&WJ line, some services being handled by Glasgow & South Western engines, whilst others were worked by Caledonian locomotives. Two G&SWR engines employed regularly on the line were Smellie's '119' class 'Greenock Bogies' Nos. 87 and 88, which often headed the Belfast boat trains between Carlisle and Stranraer.

Other G&SWR engines employed on the Portpatrick & Wigtownshire route during the Pregrouping era included the Manson '8' class

4–4–0s, the first of which had been built at Kilmarnock in 1892. Fifty-seven 'Manson Bogies' were eventually built, and numerous examples appeared on the P&WJ route – among them No. 214, which was involved in accidents at New Galloway and near Creetown in 1913 and 1919 respectively. The '8' class were followed by other Manson 4–4–0 designs, among them the '240' class, which were regularly employed on the important boat train workings between Stranraer and Carlisle.

Freight traffic was typically handled by six-coupled tender locomotives such as the familiar Caledonian Railway 'Jumbo' 0–6–0s, which were destined to enjoy a very long association with the Dumfries to Stranraer route. These ubiquitous 'Standard Goods' locomotives were designed by Dugald Drummond, the first examples being built in 1883. The class was perpetuated by Lambie and McIntosh, and they could be seen on the P&WJ line throughout the LMS and BR periods.

The London Midland & Scottish Railway inherited a large number of different locomotive classes from its various constituents, many of these diverse types being of 19th Century vintage. In an attempt to introduce greater uniformity, the company decided to scrap many Pregrouping classes en masse. This policy was based upon cost reduction for maintenance and the need to reduce the number of spare parts, in particular boilers that had to be held in stock. This policy led to the wholesale extinction of many former Glasgow & South Western classes. On the other hand, some of the numerically-strong Caledonian classes were selected as LMS standard types and, as a result of this decision, former Caledonian 4–4–0 locomotives replaced G&SWR classes on the Carlisle to Stranraer route.

In the late 1920s, ex-Caledonian Pickersgill 4–4–0s Nos. 14492 and 14493 were noted at work on the P&WJ route, whilst Caledonian 0–6–0s such as No. 17440 were favoured for local goods and branch-line duties. The most significant development on the P&WJ route during the LMS era was, however, the appearance of Midland-type locomotives. Midland or LNWR engines had not worked on the line through Castle Douglas in the Pregrouping period, but they became particularly common after the LMS decided to adopt Midland classes such as the 'Class 2P' 4–4–0s as standard types. Engines of this type employed on the line in LMS days included Nos. 600, 645 and 646.

On 30th December 1935, two 'Class 2P' 4–4–0s were derailed at speed as they were heading the Belfast boat express across the Ken Viaduct, to the west of Castle Douglas. All seven coaches left the rails, but happily, there were few injuries – most of the passengers having been asleep in their bunks at the time of the accident. Fowler 'Class 2P' 4–4–0s remained regular performers on the Portpatrick & Wigtownshire line for many years, some examples noted on the line during the British

Railways era being Nos. 40566, 40600, 40611, 40616, 40623, 40638 and 40664.

Another Midland locomotive class chosen as a standard type during the early LMS period were the 3-cylinder 'Class 4P' Compounds. These had been the best engines on the pre-1923 Midland Railway, and it was decided that further Compounds would be built. The new engines soon appeared in Scotland, two examples noted at Stranraer during the 1930s being Nos. 916 and 1179. At first, these Midland-style 4–4–0s were used mainly on the Glasgow to Stranraer route, but they later became regular performers on the P&WJ line; Nos. 40577, 41092, 41099, 41127 and 41132 were among the engines seen on the route in BR days.

In 1934, Stanier introduced his two-cylinder 'Class 5' 4–6–0s, which were the first 4–6–0s to be constructed by the LMS for mixed traffic working. These engines were clearly inspired by the highly successful GWR 'Hall' class, and no less than 842 'Class Fives' were eventually built. The new 4–6–0 engines first appeared on the P&WJ route around 1939 and, in the next few years, they became the predominant form of motive power on passenger services on the Stranraer line. Numerous examples appeared on the route at different times, some random examples from the British Railways era being Nos. 44707, 44721, 44791, 44884, 44993, 44995, 44996, 44957, 45432, 45460, 45469, 45125, 45254, 45384 and 45471.

Until the advent of the 'Class 5' 4–6–0s, the Hughes-Fowler 'Crab' class 2–6–0s were probably the most useful locomotives employed between Dumfries and Stranraer. Introduced in 1926, these general-purpose 2–6–0s had a wide route availability and, as mixed traffic locomotives, they were equally at home on passenger or freight duties. Some examples recorded on the P&WJ route at various times during the BR period include Nos. 42749, 42905, 42908 and 42967.

Stanier 'Jubilee' class 4–6–0s appeared on the line during World War Two and throughout the British Railways period. On Sunday, 16th May 1965, for example, 'Jubilee' class locomotive No. 45573 *Newfoundland* was noted at the head of an eastbound military special conveying troops between Stranraer and Woodburn in Northumberland. Some other 'Jubilees' seen on the Portpatrick & Wigtownshire route included Nos. 45588 *Kashmir*, 45657 *Tyrwhitt*, 45704 *Leviathan* and 45718 *Dreadnought*. On 27th May 1964, sister engine No. 45629 *Straights Settlements* double-headed an excursion from Newcastle to Castle Douglas in conjunction with Stanier 'Class 5' 4–6–0 No. 44791.

Pacific locomotives, in the form of the British Railways 'Clan' class 4–6–2s, worked also over the route on a sporadic basis, some examples known to have appeared on the P&WJ line being Nos. 72005 *Clan Macgregor*, 72006 *Clan MacKenzie*, 72007 *Clan Mackintosh* and 72008 *Clan Macleod*. In August 1961, for instance, a *Railway Magazine* correspondent

recorded that Nos. 72007 and 72008 had recently worked through to Stranraer at the head of Bertram Mills Circus trains, whilst on 16th May Nos. 72006 and 72008 worked military specials from Woodburn to Stranraer.

Other British Railways Standard locomotives recorded on the line included 'Class 4MT' moguls Nos. 76001, 76072, 76073, 76074 and 76112, which were employed on main-line services between Carlisle and Stranraer, and also on the Kirkcudbright branch during its final years of operation. On 5th April 1965, for example, 'Class 4MT' 2–6–0 No. 76074 worked the 3.30 p.m. branch train from Castle Douglas and the 4.51 p.m. return working from Kirkcudbright.

Smaller 2–6–0s, such as BR Standard 'Class 2MT' moguls Nos. 78016 and 78060 and Ivatt 'Class 2MT' 2–6–0 No. 46467, often worked Whithorn branch freight services, whilst BR Standard 'Class 4MT' 2–6–4Ts, such as Nos. 80023, 80061, 80117 and 80119, appeared on the Kirkcudbright branch and also on the Portpatrick & Wigtownshire main line.

Older Pregrouping locomotives were not entirely displaced by the more modern LMS or BR classes, and a few former Caledonian engines could still be seen on the P&WJ route in the 1950s. In July 1956, for example, Caledonian 'Standard Goods' 0–6–0 No. 57349 was noted at work on a Dumfries to Kirkcudbright passenger service. Veteran Caledonian 0–6–0s remained a feature of the local railway scene almost to the very end, and as late as September 1963 it was reported that 'Standard Goods' engines Nos. 57296, 57302 and 57375 were still at work in the area, together with McIntosh '812' class engine No. 57600 and Pickersgill 0–6–0 No. 57661.

The lengthy journey from Dumfries to Stranraer meant that tender engines predominated on the P&WJ route. There was, nevertheless, a requirement for one or two smaller tank locomotives such as McIntosh '92' class 0–4–4T No. 55125, which was stationed at Stranraer for service on the Portpatrick branch, and worked the last train on 4th February 1950. Shunting duties at Stranraer were undertaken by former Caledonian 0–6–0Ts, three examples recorded on these humble duties during the 1950s being McIntosh 0–6–0Ts Nos. 56234, 56302 and 56372.

A description of the line will follow in Part 2.

LMS JOURNAL INDEX

Some time ago the LMS Society undertook to produce an index for *LMS Journal* and although some progress has been made, much remains to be done to complete the index for the editions published to date. I have asked the Society to let me have an update of progress which can be published in *LMS Journal* No. 20.   *(Editor)*

BRITISH TRANSPORT COMMISSION

A. YEAMAN
District Traffic Superintendent

Telephone
18?0
? lines

Our Reference

Your Reference

PX.15996

BRITISH RAILWAYS

DISTRICT TRAFFIC SUPERINTENDENT
SCOTTISH REGION
INVERNESS

21st March, 1957.

D. Swift, Esq.,
    13, Usher Street,
        LINCOLN.

Dear Sir,

   I am in receipt of your
letter of 18th March and wish to inform you
that while passengers may travel ih Brake
Van of Goods Trains when there is no
convenient Passenger Train Service, such
travel is not encouraged by British Railways.

   The passenger must pay the
Ordinary First Class Single Fare and no
exception is made in favour of the Holder
of return or composite tickets.

   The passenger travels at his
own risk and I attach a request form setting
out the conditions upon which such a
concession is granted.

   I regret no permission can be
given to travel on Branch Lines which are
closed to Passenger Train Services.

      Yours faithfully,

      A. YEAMAN
      PER

Letter dated 21st March 1957 from the District Traffic Superintendent of British Railways, Scottish Region at Inverness, confirming that it was still possible for passengers to travel in the brake van of a freight train in certain conditions.
COLLECTION P. TATLOW

Passengers Travelling by Freight Train

by PETER TATLOW

MOST readers will probably realise that non-railwaymen responsible for livestock in transit by rail were allowed, on payment of an appropriate fare or depending on a minimum number of beasts conveyed, to travel on freight trains subject to special conditions. What may not be so well known is that, in certain circumstances, members of the general public could, with official sanction, travel in the brake van of an LMS freight train.

Before the almost universal ownership of cars, at some places, such as northern Scotland, the railway was the only means of communication over even quite short distances and even doctors in general practice might depend upon the local railway to reach patients in urgent need of their care. An example was crossing from one side of the River Oykell over the high viaduct between the station of Culrain and Invershin, a distance of a mere 772 yards, or less than half a mile, for which a fare of one half penny used to be charged, when travelling by conventional passenger train. Nonetheless, in such remote regions, passenger services were infrequent, but other possible methods of travel existed.

The LMS *Appendix to the Working Timetable for the Northern Division, March 1937 until further notice*, states on page 175 under local instructions for Wick, Inverness and Stanley and branches, the following:

'RULE 9 – PASSENGERS TRAVELLING BY FREIGHT TRAIN

Passengers may travel in the brake van of freight trains, when there is no convenient passenger train service, provided

1) That the passenger making application to travel by a freight train undertakes all risks and dangers of conveyance, and that the Company shall not be liable for any loss or injury occurring to him, however caused, and that he signs the special conditions printed on tickets to be used for the purpose.

2) That the passenger pays the ordinary first class fare – no exception being made in favour of holders of return or composition tickets.

3) That the freight train is timed to stop at the stations from and to which the passenger desires to travel.

The ticket must be shown to the guard before the train starts, and collected by him at destination and sent to District Goods and Passenger Manager attached to train journal.'

Prior to that, the 15th April 1907 (p 4) 1st June 1916 (p 4) and 1st May 1920 (p 7) editions of the Highland Railway Appendices to the WWT, as a modifica-

The sort of goods brake van one might have travelled in. No. 294071 was an ex-Highland Railway 20-ton 20ft long, six-wheeled van. Note the raised lookout, as yet without a ramped central roof over the steps up to the lookout seat, intended to prevent the guard's head striking the corner of the roof.
COLLECTION W. O. STEEL

tion of Rule 20(b), said more or less the same thing, although it was expressed in terms of goods, rather than freight trains, together with an additional paragraph:

'The fare charged must be inserted by the Booking Clerk, with ink, at the foot of the ticket issued to the Passenger in the space at the left-hand corner, the word 'Fare' being written before the figures.'

The last paragraph was replaced by:

'The Ticket, or authority to travel, must be shown to the Guard of the Train by which the holder travels before the train starts, whether Goods or Live Stock, and collected at destination and sent to Traffic Manager attached to Train Journal, in which a note of the circumstances must be recorded.'

The first HR 1897 Appendix merely states:

'Stationmasters must be particular in seeing that any passenger wishing to travel by Goods Train is made thoroughly conversant with the conditions under which the Company are prepared to so convey him, and that he signs the same.'

H. A. Valance asserts in his book, *The Highland Railway*, that the arrangement had been in use since the 1890s specifically on the overnight goods train from Wick to Helmsdale, where the passenger could make a connection with the early morning train to Inverness. The appendices do not appear to restrict the routes, other than north of Stanley Jct, although one imagines that only on the Further North line from Inverness was the passenger service sufficiently infrequent to warrant allowing passengers on freight trains. Nonetheless, the arrangement continued into early BR days, as the letter dated 21st March 1957 demonstrates, and indeed, as some of the tickets illustrated show, for another decade or so, by which time freight trains in the region were becoming rather few. It is known that a similar arrangement applied on former Great North of Scotland territory, although in this case a separate indemnity in the form of a small card had to be signed by the intending passenger and that was still being used up to 1969.

For my part, like I imagine many others, I can only wish we had found out about this delightful arrangement in time to have taken advantage of it before it was too late.

References:

Highland Railway, *Appendices to the working timetable*, 15th April, 1st June 1916 and 1st May 1920 ufn.

LMS, *Sectional appendix to the working timetables, Northern Division*, March 1937, ERO 46485.

Valance H A, *The Highland Railway*, 2nd Edition, David & Charles, 1963.

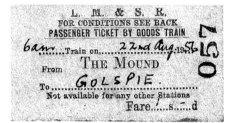

An LMS passenger ticket by goods train for 6.0 a.m. train on 22nd August 1956 from The Mound to Golspie.
COLLECTION GLYN WAITE

On the reverse side was the wording of the indemnity to be signed by the intending passenger, in this case a D. Capper.
COLLECTION GLYN WAITE

Admittedly the railways had been nationalised by 18th August 1956, but this LMS ticket had been made out to Nethy Bridge on the former LNER North Scottish Area.
COLLECTION GLYN WAITE

COLLECTION JOHN ROAKE

L M S TIMES

LMS JOURNAL No. 11

In the editorial of LMS Journal No. 11, I used the expression 'hopping the twig' (although it was spelt as ''hoping') and asked if anyone could throw any light on the origin of the term. I am glad to say that Peter Kibble has provided the answer and said he was familiar with it when he lived in London, where, in certain parts of the capital, it means not falling over your feet, not tripping up, everything is all right. This certainly fits in with the circumstances when it was used and the outlook of Driver Smith who, when we were running well, no shortage of steam, the fire was in good shape and boiler level where it should be, would say 'We're hopping the twig.'   *(Editor)*

LMS JOURNAL No. 15

Further to my article on the Mansfield to Rolleston Junction line, two additional and pertinent pieces of information should be added:

Page 53 — 'although the 1912 Midland Railway map of the Mansfield district shows that running rights were in force over the LD&ECR as far as Ollerton'. Subsequently I have discovered that such running rights applied to two local passenger services for workmen.

Page 38 refers to the construction of the Mansfield Railway and its connections to various collieries in the immediate vicinity. Although independent, the Mansfield Railway was the brainchild of the Bolsover Colliery Company and served four of its six collieries. That there was a close alliance with the Great Central Railway at the time of its construction was due to a commitment to transport some half a million tons of coal annually from these pits to Immingham for export or bunkering. There were several directors common to both companies.

Keith Turton

Regarding the back cover picture of splitting distants, on the offchance that no one has as yet written with details of the location and an explanation, here is my offering:

The location is Winwick Quay, looking north. The photographer would now have the M62 Motorway behind him. The lines from left to right are: Down Slow, Down Fast, Up Fast and Up Slow.

The signal on the left has the splitting distants for the Down Slow. Left arm to take the Vulcan Branch to Earlestown Triangle with the LNWR Manchester—Liverpool main line. Trains taking this route would be/are North Wales/Chester—Manchester and in the past the to St. Helens push-pull. Right arm (off) to take main line to Golbourne Junction, Wigan, Preston, etc. Up distant is for Up Fast.

The signal on the right provides splitting distants for the Up Fast for routes mentioned above and the distant is for the Up Slow.

R. J. Longworth
Altrincham

Thank you. I knew a reader would supply the answer.   *(Editor)*

Contrary to the statement on page 1 that the Fowler 2—6—2Ts did not work on the Midland Division, Nos. 15520-39 (later 21-40) fitted with condensing apparatus spent their working lives (with a few exceptions) in the London district of the Midland Division at Kentish Town, Cricklewood and St. Albans and were a familiar sight all round the capital on transfer workings as well as on the MR proper. The last to be withdrawn was No. 40022 from Cricklewood in December 1962.

Stephen Summerson
Luton

With reference to the 'Train acceleration policy' article on pages 3—12 inclusive, may I offer the following extract from the *Glasgow Herald* of Thursday, 28th May 1931, page 6.

Railway Speed-Up
LMS Summer Services Acceleration

LMS summer train services which come into operation on 20th July, were to be both speeded up and intensified. Each of the week travel arrangements had been the subject of special attention, with the result that numerous trains, which last year were reserved for excursion passengers only, were this year included in the timetable, and would be available for ordinary, tourist and weekend ticket passengers. The running of semi-expresses and local trains had also been the subject of expert analysis, and in the summer timetable 778 trains would show a total acceleration of 2,552 minutes — a saving of nearly 43 hours in travel time every day. While the main alterations came into force on 20th July, additional trains were scheduled to run during June. These included the following:

Commencing 6th June — a new Saturday only restaurant car express would leave Glasgow Central and Edinburgh Princes Street at 10.45 a.m., arriving London at 7.30 p.m., and calling at Carlisle, Warrington, Crewe and Rugby.

Commencing 1st June — the 5.10 p.m. from Glasgow St. Enoch would arrive at Stranraer at 8.15 p.m. — an acceleration of 20 minutes over the same service last year.

Changes affecting Scotland

Particulars of the principal alterations affecting Scotland, which would take effect as from 20th July were:

The 9.20 a.m. express from Glasgow St. Enoch to London St. Pancras — 2.30 p.m. ex Leeds — would travel via and call at Sheffield at 3.18 p.m. and depart at 3.23 p.m. This would provide a through service from Glasgow to Sheffield and give a new afternoon service from Sheffield to London. The arrival time at St. Pancras — 6.35 p.m. — would remain unaltered.

The 10.00 a.m. 'Royal Scot' express from London Euston to Rugby, Crewe, Carlisle, Glasgow Central and Edinburgh Princes Street would cease calling at Rugby, Crewe and Carlisle, and run from London to Glasgow and Edinburgh, with a stop at Carlisle to change engines only.

A restaurant car express would leave London Euston at 10.05 a.m. for Aberdeen, Dundee and Stranraer, calling at Rugby, Crewe and Carlisle.

'The Royal Highlander'

The popular first and third class sleeping car express, 'The Royal Highlander', would leave London Euston at 7.20 p.m., Saturdays excepted, for Inverness and Aberdeen, with connections to the whole of the North of Scotland.

A sleeping car express — first and third class — would leave London Euston at 7.30 p.m. for Oban daily, except Saturdays, due Oban at 9.25 a.m. It would have connections at Crianlarich with the L&NER train to Fort William. A restaurant car would be provided in the train from Stirling.

The present 7.30 p.m., Saturdays excepted, sleeping car express from London Euston to Inverness, Dundee and Aberdeen would leave Euston at 7.40 p.m., and would not convey passengers from London, but only from intermediate stations. It would cease to convey a portion for Stranraer.

Sleeping car express, Saturdays excepted, would leave London Euston at 8.00 p.m. for Stranraer, and would convey a through portion, including a sleeping-car for Turnberry via Stranraer and Girvan.

Arnold Tortorella
Glasgow

LMS JOURNAL No. 16

With reference to the 'Query Corner' on page 17, on Friday, 27th April 1928, the LMS went 'one-up' on the LNER which was to commence non-stop running between King's Cross and Edinburgh on 30th April. The LMS ran the 'Royal Scot' in two parts from Euston non-stop to Glasgow and Edinburgh. The Glasgow portion was hauled by No. 6113 *Cameronian* and the Edinburgh section by compound 4—4—0 No. 1054. *Cameronian* was coupled to a tender of greater capacity than its standard one, which is seen in this photograph, to assist the crew on this long and arduous journey.

However, the train in the picture is not likely to be the 'Royal Scot'. It has 14 bogies behind the tender and is an up Western Division express at Kenton. The building just visible above the third coach is an electricity sub-station. Just in front of it, and not visible in the published photograph, is the bridge carrying the Metropolitan and LNER (GC) Joint line over the LMS tracks. The photographer (unknown) is standing between the up and down 'new lines' electrified tracks about 850 yards south of this bridge.

M. A. Elston
Guildford

Regarding your question on page 17, I believe this to be an Up express just the London side of the GC & Met overbridge at Northwick Park/Kenton, with the Power Supply Building in the background.

Martin Higginson

Cameronian is on an up Western Division express near Kenton, seen running with one of three specially modified ex-MR Deeley tenders. The outwards-extended coal rails on the three tenders had been added to allow an increased coal load of 9 tons to be carried, in readiness for

ORDER NO. 7050 - Sheet No. 1
Alteration to Coal Capacity of one Tender
(taken off old 990 class Engines which
have been broken up).

A test is to be made which will necessitate this
tender carrying 1½ tons more coal than at present, and the
following drawings have been issued for the material to be
prepared and the tender to be modified to give the extra coal
capacity.-

RS-818 Alteration to tender coping (1 copy Tender Shop)
and bunker plates. (1 ", Boiler Shop)

RS-819 Feed Water handle, etc., " "

RS-821 Casing for feed valve gear.

In addition to the foregoing, it will be necessary
to provide bunker doors on the tender front to permit the
enginemen entering into the coal bunker to pull down the coal.

A list of the detail drawings is given below.

Please arrange for this work to be put in hand as
early as possible so that the material will be ready for fitting
on the tender in time for the test.

Old Drawing No.	New Drawing No.	Name of Part.	Remarks.
05-6364	RS-818	Tank Arrangement.	The coping plate is to be cut down level with the top of the 4½" beading, except round the end of the water pick-up chamber. New shovelling plate. New coping plates. New Coal Tender Bars, and supporting angles and cross stretcher plates, also bunker doors.
05-6369	RS-818	Frame Arrangement	Driver's Platform raised and plate cut as shown on casing RS-821.
	RS-819	Feed Water Handle) Hose Connection) Carrier & Clip.)	New
	RS-821	Casing to protect) feed water gear.)	New

(CONTINUED)

ORDER NO. 7050.- Sheet No. 1 Continued.

The following new parts are required and could
be taken from an order now going through.-

Old Drawing No.	Name of part	Remarks.
27-10691	Bunker Doors	New, complete. Tank front altered to suit.
27-11209	Bunker Door Details	New complete.
27-11210 RS-849 24/1/28	Fire iron Bracket	New
05-6287	Feed Valve Rod Crank Bracket Pin and Bolts $\frac{5\ CX}{12}$	New details 13,14,15 / 6287
S-2193	Flange & coupling for Steam Brake.	Flexible Pipe to be 2'7" between sleeves. New details same as O/4553.

The following are to be taken from a
"Royal Scot" tender.-

27-10945	Feed Water Connections Details 5,6,7,8,9 & 12
05-6324	The Vacuum Train Pipe, Hose and Coupling.
10-8132	Carriage Warming Pipes, Hose and Coupling.

The existing details can be used again for.-

[signature]

WORKS SUPERINTENDENT.

beating the LNER's objective of running the first non-stop train service between London and Edinburgh, well publicised to be launched on Monday, 30th April 1928.

On Friday, 27th April 1928, the LMS divided the 'Royal Scot' train into two sections — an Edinburgh portion, the second the Glasgow portion, both running non-stop after leaving Euston. Compound 4—4—0 No. 1054 was fitted with modified tender No. 2751, which had been modified after removal from a 3P 4—4—0. *Cameronian* received one of the other two modified tenders, either 2805 or 2808, both previously taken from 999 Class 4—4—0s. There was a driver and two firemen on each train.

The two non-stop runs by the LMS on the Friday immediately prior to the LNER's well planned inauguration of first non-stop running of the 'Flying Scotsman' train between King's Cross and Edinburgh on the following Monday, 30th April 1928, stole the 'non-stop express' limelight from the LNER.

Nelson Twells
Chesterfield

On page 17, No. 6113 is on an express on the up fast line south of Watford, the second non-electrified track away from the camera. I cannot, however, pinpoint the location.

The tender is T2805, one of three similar Deeley long-wheelbase tenders specially rebuilt for attachment to the two engines allocated to the celebrated non-stop runs from Euston to Glasgow and Edinburgh on 27th April 1928 (the third one was spare). These tenders were modified to O/7050 of 5th January 1928 by splaying outwards the upper side sheets of the tenders, providing new front plates with bunker doors, new rear bunker plates and coal rails between them. This increased the coal capacity from 6 to 9 tons. All had been built in 1908-9, that on No. 6113 originating with MR 990 class 4—4—0 No. 993 which had been withdrawn in January 1928. It was first allocated to Compound No. 1057 in March 1928 before being attached to No. 6113.

The engine history cards and tender history cards are confusing because they show T2805 put to No. 6113 on 6th November 1928 which clearly is incorrect. Tender 3904 is recorded as attached to No. 6113 on 27th August 1929, so assuming this is correct, the photographs must date between April 1928 and August 1929. On removal, T2805 went to Compound No. 1061 and then to Compound No. 1057 from September 1937 until withdrawal in May 1948.

Stephen Summerson
Luton

Thank you to all the other readers who came up with the same answer.
(Editor)

Sadly, this was the last letter I received from Stephen Summerson. Shortly after it arrived, I heard of his untimely death. I had known Stephen for many years and we regularly exchanged information.
Bob Essery

With reference to the article about the LNW/GN joint line, when taking photographs in the late 50s, around Northampton, I saw the train from Doncaster several times. I have a photograph of it behind WD 90064, a Doncaster engine at the time. WDs were unusual at Northampton and a Doncaster one even more so. From conversations I have had, if an Eastern loco worked through, it was always a WD due to clearance problems. I have been told that sometimes an O2 showed up which created problems as they were too wide to run through the platform roads at Northampton Castle. It is sometimes forgotten that the GN had a similar loading gauge to the GWR.

James Baxendale
Hemel Hempstead

In the LMS Signalling article on page 23, the authors state that the standard LMS frame was suitable, unlike others, to work 'Economical Facing Point Locks'. Presumably they were referring in particular to the Standard ex-Midland Railway 'Prince and Langley' lock and not in general terms? EFPLs were also, of course, used by many other companies but to a far less extent. These were as a general rule supplied by the various signalling contractors; for example, the H&B had several EFPLs worked by Saxby & Farmer 'Rocker', '1888 Duplex' and EoD locking frames. The NE successfully worked EFPLs from the various types of McKenzie & Holland locking frames.

Mick Nicholson

On page 23 of the LMS Signalling article it is stated that A. F. Bound came from the GNR, but I think you will find that, at grouping at least, he was with the GC and accounted for the signalling innovations on that line following World War One (see *A Pictorial Record of LNER Constituent Signalling*, A. A. MacLean, OPC 1983). The *Railway Year Book* for 1923, page 178, lists him as Signal Superintendent under the Engineer of the Great Central Section — A. F. Bound, MIMechE, MInstT, Guide Bridge, Manchester.

Peter Tatlow
Lymington

On page 43, the bottom two illustrations have had their captions transposed.

Jim Jackson
Newark

LMS JOURNAL No. 17

There is an error in the caption to the charming photograph on page 35, which was taken between Dingwall and Fodderty Junction. It shows a train to the Kyle, which is being banked in rear to Raven's Rock summit, and not an Inverness to Aberdeen train as suggested.

There is a photograph by R. D. Stephen showing a Skye Bogie at this exact location with a goods train. I wonder if this photograph was not taken by him or his brother, W. D. M. Stephen.

There is at least one photograph of 14412 *Ben Avon* on a Kyle train during the 1926 General Strike, which was taken by K. A. C. R. Nunn.

Richard White
Botswana

Perhaps being No. 13 in the series of line societies did the trick, but the photograph which accompanied the article about the Highland Railway Society (page 35) appeared with the wrong caption. It should have been:

'14412 *Ben Avon* hauling a train for Kyle of Lochalsh, about 1928. It is banked by a 4–4–0, most likely a Skye Bogie but possibly a Loch. The location is approaching Fodderty Junction, 2 miles out of Dingwall. The train would be banked as far as Raven's Rock. Despite this, the train only consists of a horsebox and 6 bogie coaches, with possibly another van at the rear, which seems light given the allowed load of 170 tons, and the HR's estimate of a bogie coach as amounting to 23 tons. Both LMS and Highland coaches can be identified. The photo is in the Highland Railway Society collection and came from Harold D. Bowtell but may well have been taken by R. D. Stephen.'

Perhaps this is an opportunity to expand on the working of what appears as a banked train on level track.

The line from Kyle of Lochalsh branches off the main line north from Inverness at Dingwall and heads roughly west. The first few miles are flat. The route originally sanctioned took the line through the town of Strathpeffer. Local landowners, in particular Sir William MacKenzie of Coul House, put up determined opposition and a deviation had to be sanctioned. Thus at Fodderty, 2¼ miles from Dingwall, the line swung over to the other side of the valley and started climbing for about 4 miles at a steady gradient of 1 in 50 to the summit at Raven's Rock

before descending to Garve. A station to serve Strathpeffer was built halfway up the bank and later a crossing loop was installed here. Later the people of Strathpeffer realised their loss and petitioned for a branch; this was opened from Fodderty Junction in 1885 and helped the town to develop as an important holiday destination based on its spa. In June 1911 the Highland Railway opened a large hotel there; it is still open, though these days to accommodate coach parties. When the branch opened, the original Strathpeffer station was renamed Achterneed. Fodderty Junction was a very simple single set of points without the double line junction arrangement sometimes insisted on by the Board of Trade.

The climb to Raven's Rock from the east was much harder than any other gradients on the line, so assistance became necessary. Given that there were only 3 or 4 trains a day on the line, the bankers started with the train at Dingwall, hence the sight in the photograph in question of a banked train on level ground.

Initially it appears that no special signalling arrangements were made and that the banker simply returned to Achterneed while the train continued to Garve. The banker would then be signalled in the normal way back to Dingwall. In 1921, a banking key was provided at Achterneed, to ensure that both the train and the banker cleared the section before another token was released.

A full description of the signalling arrangements is given in the Sectional Appendix to WTT for the Northern Division for March 1937 ufn. Between Dingwall and Achterneed, the banker had to be coupled to the train with vacuum pipes connected. The banking key was released from a separate instrument at Achterneed and could only be withdrawn after a tablet had been released from the instrument for the Achterneed—Garve section. Withdrawal of the banking key locked the tablet instruments and interlocked with the levers in the signal box. The banking key was given to the driver of the banker when the section tablet was handed to the train driver. When the banker returned to Achterneed, the banking token was handed back to the station master and restored to its instrument. No further tablet could be obtained until both the train tablet and the banking key had been inserted in their respective instruments. If the banking key could not be issued, the banker had to remain coupled to the train, with vacuum connections complete, until it reached Garve. These arrangements did not apply to Mixed or freight trains. These arrangements seem to have continued until the end of steam working in 1960/61. The Strathpeffer branch closed to passengers in 1946 and goods in 1951, after which the junction was removed.

The steep gradients to Raven's Rock were the cause of runaways on more than one occasion, and Achterneed station acquired trap points on both loop lines to derail anything trying to escape. These were interlocked with the token instruments for the section to Dingwall after Fodderty Junction had closed, to ensure that movements between Dingwall and Strathpeffer were protected.

For an atmospheric account of this section of the line, Peter Tatlow recounted a visit in July 1958 in 'Night on a Bare Mountain' (*Backtrack* December 1996, pp 692-7). Peter did not see any banked trains, but the heavy mid-morning train was double-headed by a Black Five and Caley 4–4–0 and the latter returned light from Garve.

Regarding the photograph on page 59, John Edgington phoned to say that he thought it was taken from the ex-L&NWR bridge at Washwood Heath, when the photographer was looking north, with the line to the Metro Cammel works on the right. He is quite correct. The scene looked familiar but I never saw Washwood Heath from that angle. To the left is the front fan of sidings whilst in the centre we can see the back fan of departure sidings. *(Editor)*

The caption to the picture on page 63, 'London to Birmingham Express' should read 'Lincoln to Birmingham Express'.

Jim Jackson
Newark

On page 73 of the article, 'My Railway Experiences', it should read 'Macclesfield Central Station, a joint LMS/LNER station', not Hibel Road.

John Hulme
Leeds

'Mosell — Give Matter Special Attention', page 16 of *LMS Journal* No. 17, although the 'Telegraph' has long fallen out of use, several of the code words are still used verbally. For example, locally the expression 'Cape' is used and understood by all when referring to a cancelled train. As an aside, the last railway telegraph circuit in the UK was between Newark South signal box and Doncaster telegraph office. This fell out of use as late as 18th October 1976.

Mick Nicholson
Hull